Storms... in Our Lives

How God Brought Us Through

Hannah T. Merritt

iUniverse, Inc.
New York Bloomington

Storms... in Our Lives
How God Brought Us Through

iUniverse books may be ordered through booksellers or by contacting:

iUniverse
1663 Liberty Drive
Bloomington, IN 47403
www.iuniverse.com
1-800-Authors (1-800-288-4677)

Because of the dynamic nature of the Internet, any Web addresses or links contained in this book
may have changed since publication and may no longer be valid. The views expressed in this work
are solely those of the author and do not necessarily reflect the views of the publisher, and the
publisher hereby disclaims any responsibility for them.

ISBN: 978-1-4502-2173-3 (pbk)
ISBN: 978-1-4502-2175-7 (cloth)
ISBN: 978-1-4502-2174-0 (ebook)

Printed in the United States of America

iUniverse rev. date: 6/8/10

Acknowledgments

I thank God, the Giver and Sustainer of life. I would like to acknowledge Mr. Gregg Barnett who obtained the necessary equipment that I may compile my information. I am very appreciative for the precious gifts: my children. They are indeed gifts from God. Lydia is likened to a precious stone. She has performed a priceless part in my endeavor. Without her, I would not have attained my goal as timely. She has shared her skills and talents unselfishly and has contributed many hours giving assistance to me despite her busy schedule. She shall be blessed for we find in life what we put into it. Although Sari resides in another city, she too has supported this effort and never ceased to believe in me. I am thankful for my children and their support.

Dedication

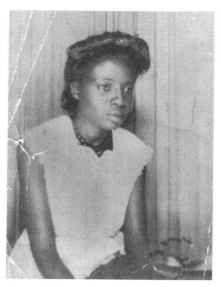

Auntie Susie B. Clarkson-Taylor

This book is dedicated to my beloved Auntie Susie. She is one of three children. Her brother, Ellis Clarkson and my mother, Annie Clarkson-Turner have gone to be with the Lord. I am truly grateful that God has allowed Auntie to spend many years with us. She is a beacon in our lives despite medical problems, which complicated most of her adult life. Wisdom allows her to share information from the past, and she brings laughter with her jokes. Family and friends call her *"blessed."*

Introductory Song
"SOMEDAY"
Beams of heaven as I go,
Through the wilderness below, …

Written in 1906
By
Charles Albert Tindley
1851-1933

Depicts the Narrative,
Storms…
In Our Lives

Introduction

Storms…In Our Lives is an inspirational narrative, which I hope some can identify with and others may learn from it. It is unique because it is a mixture of *historical events, life happenings, and a reminder of Biblical words of encouragement.*

My intent is to inform children, adolescents, and young adults of hardships, which our ancestors endured, and tell them about my experiences. Should they face similar situations, I hope they will reflect on how I made it day by day through the *storms of disappointments.* I survived with God's help and they will too.

Occasionally, I used metaphors to make comparisons. I reflected on childhood experiences of living with my abusive father. Mother was quiet, loving, but passive. She believed that God would make a way somehow. Country living included working on a farm and playing in the sand. We played with dolls, which we made from empty wooden thread spools or soda pop bottles. We utilized baling twine as hair for the dolls.

After retiring for the day, I slept in a bed between two of my sisters, or on a quilt on the floor. The little shotgun house had only three rooms! No one considered square footage. All of those thoughts and many more occurred to me. It was time to compile the stunning information in book form. God has brought us all the way, and I would like to share my story. I recalled numerous experiences of trials, tribulations, good times, and bad times.

The Master of the universe has allowed me to live to be able to tell this story. *"Ye observe days, and months, and times, and years."* (Galatians 4:10

KJV) By the sequential order of them, there has been a change in my life. I perceive it is time to share my thoughts and life happenings with those who will read this narrative. Perhaps someone will be touched, steered in the right direction, and motivated to stay on the straight and narrow pathway.

This authentic report is a narrative, which includes a bundle of sadness. It is wrapped with death, tragedy, and connected with humor that cannot be suppressed. Moreover, the reader will discover several episodes in which humor is distinguished. Many may find this story amazing in part and difficult to fathom.

Inventors made notable contributions to society. Therefore, I reflected on inventions in this story because we did not always have the conveniences, which are available to us today.

Table of Contents

Chapter 1

The Beginning of Terror

Annie (BB) Clarkson and Gemstone (Pharaoh) Turner were married in Grand Bayou, Louisiana. It is a small plantation, which is located in Red River Parish about thirty-seven miles south of Shreveport, Louisiana. Highway 1 was the route to travel for medical care, food, and clothing. However, very few families owned automobiles in 1938. Those were the days of horse and buggy, or mule and wagon for many. The nearest school was located just off a dirt road about eight miles away. Mom, like a typical new bride, thought she was entering into a loving relationship with a husband who loved her.

World War II began in 1939 just months after Mother's first child was born. Family draftees for military service were aware that the war opened the Atomic Age, and Japan attacked Pearl Harbor in 1941. At that time, Mother had given birth to three children. Her second child lived only three days.

The United States went to war. Franklin Delano Roosevelt was President of the United States when Dad received orders to go to the United States Navy to serve his country. Uncle J. Tyson received orders to go to the Army. Dad said, "I only served 'bout one year 'cause the war ended. During that time I was in the South Pacific and was injured while transporting supplies." He received a honorable discharge.

Remarkable Delivery

I was born on January 31, 1945 in Grand Bayou, Louisiana. I can imagine it was cold, the winter season. However, it was a beautiful time of the year to perform artistic works. The clock was ticking and every moment was precious. The same is true today. At the appointed time, I was born to my parents' surprise, a *big baby girl*.

Mother did not know my exact weight because a midwife delivered me. No one was there to capture the moment on film, not even with a camera. There was no crowd, not even a trio to kneel in prayer. No minister was there to ask God's blessings on my life, and no one shed tears for me. Moreover, we should cry when one is born because he enters the world of trials and tribulations. We should rejoice when one die because he leaves his troubles behind and his debt is paid in full. Most people do the opposite.

The midwife did not make a public announcement, nor did she post a banner. The Captain blew the whistle and the race began. Only He knows how long this journey will last. We learned from the book of Job, *Man that is born of a woman is of a few days and full of trouble.*

Job 14:1 (KJV)

Mrs. Winnie Stewart delivered me into this world of many unknown challenges. Her services were in demand. I am sure many mothers appreciated her devotion and willingness to perform such a task in a remarkable manner. Certainly, it was a blessing that Mother knew such a skillful woman, and she was available. Mrs. Stewart was able to do what many do not have the courage to do. Even though she did not have modern day equipment, after the final analysis she could relax with a smile. Thank God, our Creator. Mrs. Stewart apparently did a good job with the guidance of Jehovah, Master of the Universe. He willed it so, and nothing is too hard for God. I made my entrance by the hands of Mrs. Stewart who left me with a perfect belly button. Midwives have performed deliveries since the book of beginning (Genesis). The task is still noteworthy.

During those days, women placed a fifty-cent piece in a cotton bandage and used it to cover the baby's navel. The bandage held the infant's stomach tight when he cried, and the navel did not protrude. Bird eye cotton diapers were used. Mothers also placed a piece of lead on a string and tied it around the infant's neck after he started to teeth. They were not aware of teething biscuits during those days.

Astrologers study the positions of the moon. Many believe in horoscopes and think signs of the zodiac determine one's personality. Astrologers use a chart, which consist of twelve sections. According to their chart, I was born under the sign of Aquarius, the water bearer but I chose my own sign, the rugged *"cross on which Christ was crucified."* One day I will exchange it for a crown.

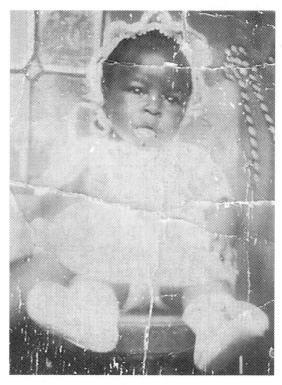

Mom's baby girl

Customarily, someone carried each newborn baby around the house. Our ancestors thought the baby would grow up to be like that person. Sometimes there were several volunteers, but the mother carefully chose one. I cannot say the tradition had any merit whatsoever. Nevertheless, grown-ups seem to believe that it did. Women were not allowed to leave home within six weeks after giving birth. They were told that it was a health concern.

Mrs. Mary Kemp was a friend to my mother. She was concerned enough about me to become my godmother and I was fortunate to have her in my life. Times were tough and Mom needed all the help she could get.

Difficulty of childbirth since the fall of man

Unto the woman God said, *I will greatly multiply thy sorrow and thy conception; in sorrow, thou shall bring forth children…*

Genesis 3:16 (KJV)

Labor is the process of childbirth, and a complex interaction of multiple factors is the response to the onset of labor. Scripture tells us:

… Rachel travailed, and she had hard labor. And it came to pass, when she was *in hard labor, that the midwife said unto her, fear not; thou shall have this son also.*

Genesis 35: 16 - 17 (KJV)

Rachel died after she gave birth to her son, who lived. Therefore, we should not take childbirth lightly. Yet, some women gave birth to as many as fifteen children. Contraceptives were not heard of as they are today and some women preferred to have children, but they were barren. We did not hear about adoption agencies, or foster parents.

Because of new technology, man may utilize modern equipment but we know God is in control. Man has become so wise he can make a *robot* but he cannot give it life. It will only be an animated machine.

Grandma, Dad's Mother

We lived with my dad's mother for a while. One summer day she was in the kitchen cooking and we were sitting on the floor with our backs against the wall. We were sitting quietly while observing from a distance. I am sure we watched her *every move*. Grandma was quiet too. I do not know what she was thinking, but she did not even hum a tune. Many of our elders hummed or sang an old one-hundred hymn while cooking, or just working. Grandma definitely believed *everybody should work*! Strangely, I do not recall a single song, which Grandma sang at any time.

She made biscuits, and as I recalled she gave Ruth one biscuit and said to her, "*Give them chullen a piece of it.*" Ruth followed instructions. She divided the biscuit into three pieces. We ate the sample and waited patiently for more. Grandma was a mean woman.

"Why did she give the three of us one biscuit together?," I asked Ruth.

Ruth did not have a clue because she did not answer me. I thought that was a stingy sample of a snack. Perchance Grandma knew we were *hungry* and a piece of bread is better than no bread at all. I can visualize people starving in other countries. They long to receive a little piece of bread. One day an old man who was a family member came by and brought a bucket of food, beans and cornbread for us. We were mistreated and evidently, he knew. I am a living witness that God will provide for His children. I was too young to understand what was going on, but Paula told me Dad took us from our mother and left us with his mother. I do not know if Mother did something wrong, and I do not know the length of time we were apart.

Mom's Character Traits

Mother was a very dedicated, hard worker, who sacrificed much for her children. She was also very artistic or perhaps I should say gifted with a talent to sew. She fashioned our little wardrobes and I thank God for her. She did not have Butterick, Simplicity, McCall or Vogue Patterns. She cut and sewed garments after observation of clothes in catalogs. That was truly a gift. Many times, we would have gone without certain things if it had not been for her talent and devotion to her little ones. Mother was appreciative for clothes and shoes, which were given to us. Other children were fortunate or blessed with new wardrobes. Therefore, they did not need *secondhand clothes*. Oh, but we wore them until they were no longer presentable! They were passed down from one child to the other.

Mother worked by the day for the owners of the plantation for example, she cooked, cleaned house, and ironed. She was their maid. We picked strawberries when they were in season to help make ends meet. Sometimes even the meal of the day was strawberries with sugar and cream. Mother was a good cook when groceries were in supply. However, most times they were scarce. I recall the raccoon, which resembles a big cat. Mother baked a raccoon, placed it on a platter, and arranged baked sweet potatoes around it. I cannot describe the taste but as I remember, the dark meat was good. I suppose Dad had gone hunting, or maybe someone gave the "*coon*" to him. Nevertheless, he owned a shotgun and I believe it was a double barrel. Dad did not own a gun case to store the gun away safely. He placed it behind a door or in a corner of the house. We knew that it was not a toy! To play with it would have meant our lives were in the pathway of danger.

Mother prepared meals on her job, and many times, we ate the leftovers. Sometimes we did not have leftovers. We ate cornbread and milk from a bowl as if it were cereal. The objective was to *survive*! We did not always have what we wanted. We ate what Mother provided for us and God spared our lives.

The table is spread with food fit for a king

Mother "*dear*" never went to school of cosmetology but she was a beautician! She did very well. That required skill or mastery and she knew how to survive. She earned a few dollars by styling hair. She comb pressed it and use the curlers to pull it even straighter. Then she curled it all over, and sometimes she did something special, "*temple curls.*" Today, we call them sister curls. Thank God for Madam C.J. Walker, who invented the process of straightening hair for black women. We commend Walter Sammons for his invention of the *comb* and Lydia O. Newman for the *hairbrush*. Thank God for the black inventors. Mother had all girls so she comb pressed our hair and curled a bang in front. It was a *big bang*! Others saw our hair styled and came by to get theirs done. Mother earned a few dollars by operating a beauty shop in our home. That meant bread and milk for another day.

"Peanut" @ age 5yrs.

Some may speculate about Mother's schooling, but she could read and write the English language and her penmanship were very legible. She had parents who were concerned and they sent her to school. She went to a little wooden schoolhouse. I believe in the nineteenth century almost all the *impetus* for setting up schools came from the *churches*. Mother had a good foundation and God given talents. Her parents were not financially able to send her to trade school. Mother's father could read and write and he instilled in her the importance of being *self-supportive*. He taught her with that in mind. I know most parents help their children even after they have grown to adulthood. Grandfather sent Mother a few dollars occasionally in the form of a money order. He knew her financial situation was almost unbearable.

Application for Money Order

Dad was not a good provider, nor was he a good father. In addition, he did not get much education. That was not his fault, but sometimes *common sense* outweighs book sense. Many men did not get an education. They learned not only to survive but also to *thrive!* Abraham Lincoln became the sixteenth president of the United States of America. He was one of the truly great men of all time. He said of himself, *"When I came of age I did not know much. Still somehow, I could read, write and cipher to the Rule of Three; but that was all."* However, God made a way. Greatness is measured far beyond knowledge, which is obtained from studying books.

Hardships

As my mind traveled back in time, I recalled many hardships and disappointments. Sometimes it is good to look back and remember from whence we came. We also need to research our roots. It just might help us to be humble and grateful, but sometimes it is depressing and we do not want to look back, nor remember our past. However, I looked down the rough road, which was filled with manifold obstacles. I very clearly pictured hurdles and turns, one after another. One may liken it to a *wilderness*, which consists of pebbles and sharp objects of many kinds. Danger was lurking in our path.

It was difficult to travel because with every step there was rubble. However, I thank God for a praying mother. We kept traveling and her prayer was in essence, "Oh Lord, guide my feet in a peaceful way. Turn my dark nights into a day of deliverance." There were many long days and dark nights when we were with the "*task master.*" Nevertheless, God kept us. In addition, it is no wonder slaves hummed many tunes. I believe they prayed and I can imagine they cried, and cried some more.

> When we noticed dark clouds forming and strong winds blowing, we ran for cover. We knew a storm was coming our way.

> "Cover the mirrors with a bed sheet and sit down and be quiet," Mother said.
> "The Lord is doing His work," She continued.
> Children made jokes when they heard thunder roar, "God is moving His furniture around."

For some reason Mother opened her big Bible and placed it on the table. I do not recall any particular book or scripture, which she opened it to, but my thought is the following scripture.

He that dwelleth in the secret place of the most High shall abide under the shadow of the Almighty. I will say of the Lord, He is my refuge and my fortress: my God; in him will I trust.

Psalm 91: 1-2 (KJV)

HOLY BIBLE

That passage of scripture is about security and trusting God for protection. The believer in God will find comfort to relieve stress *in times of storms*. God is our shelter from the storms. God is our Watchman and nothing can harm us when we are under His mighty hand unless He permits it.

We heard loud thunder and we saw lighting flashing. We huddled closely together like little chicks under the wings of a hen. If we were in bed at night Mother would say, "You'll get up and put your clothes on." We did not understand why she told us to get dressed. Later, I realized she wanted us to be prepared to do whatever was necessary at that time. Perhaps there was a need to get dressed in the event that we were to leave the house, and I have no idea of where we would have gone. I do recall something about a storm house, but I do not remember if one was underground in our yard. Sometimes storms demolished homes as they do today. Maybe they were *tornadoes* but we did not hear that word during those days.

Mother prayed and her prayer was not just for her peace of mind but for the sake of her little ones as well. Surely, there was a star of hope. She could see further than we could. She had wisdom and she kept in touch with the Giver and Sustainer of life. Mother could not give up. She was our provider and caregiver. Thus, she could not quit because we were relying upon her. Sometimes life seemed to deal her *a dirty hand*. She had to play that hand and hope for the best results. She wrestled to retain what was rightfully her own and *agonized* with oppositions. Sometimes her plans were destroyed and she grasped for straws, which were broken in the process because they were weak. She shed many tears because of *sinful acts*. Thus in this life, she had trials. The storms of life kept on raging. Many times, she was swept off her feet by disappointments and the place in which she landed was hard and very uncomfortable, but she had *resilience!*

Jesus is perfect and He endured trials and tribulations. He was scorned and denied, yet He went about doing good for humankind.

...in me, ye might have peace. In the world, ye shall have tribulation: but be of good cheer; I have overcome the world.

John 16:33 (KJV)

Jesus can identify with all our pain and suffering. We know there will be no peace without the *"Prince of Peace."* We also know He will keep us in perfect peace if we keep our minds stayed on Him. We must understand perfect peace. It is that tranquility which frees our mind from fear and worry. Paul wrote, *be careful for nothing; but in every thing by prayer and supplication with thanksgiving let your requests be made known to God.* He told us not to worry, but go to God in prayer. When we pray we should tell God all about our troubles. Even though nothing is hidden from Him. Put everything in His hands. And the peace of God, which passes all understanding, shall keep our hearts and minds through Christ Jesus. His peace guards our hearts and minds, but we must be careful not to allow evil thoughts to penetrate our minds. We are not able to understand everything but we can focus on good things. God is all knowing, wise, and His peace is perfect. His peace surpasses our little understanding! Jesus is our friend.

Joseph Scriven penned the song, *"What a Friend We Have in Jesus."* It is a good thing to sing it today, tomorrow, and as long as we live. It is inspirational.

We had many *wilderness experiences* and sometimes our focus was misdirected. It is easy to be temporarily distracted when fathers are enraged, mothers displaced, and children denied…Those are weights, which easily beset us. But God will take care of you.

Chapter 2

King "Cotton Picking" Time

Under Pressure

In 1949, Cotton crops were plentiful throughout the state. Farmers looked forward to cultivating and harvesting the fluffy white crops. They no doubt waited with great excitement and anticipation in hopes of lining their pockets with cash. According to what we heard family members say, cotton was "*king.*" Plantation owners were eager to assign families to work specific sections of a field. Cotton was even more plentiful in the State of Arkansas. Dad heard the news and raced to settle in Wilson, Arkansas. My big sister recall living among Spanish speaking people was quite a change from the life to which she was accustomed. However, we settled down and began to do the work, which we had moved there to do. We did a good job and our dad always bragged about how much cotton his family picked on a daily or weekly basis. Ruth did a very good job. It was because she was afraid of the consequences of not doing well. The pressure was on! Esther was afraid of "*worms.*" Therefore, she could not stay focused. Dad whipped her many times because she did not come up to his expectations. There were times when she stood still and observed the birds as they were gliding through the air. It seemed as if she had forgotten her *real purpose* for being there. Dad used excessive force to remind her.

"*You out heah to pick cotton,*" Dad said in a loud commanding voice.

I recall, Esther did not say a word and she was so pitiful.

"Fill that sack up, "Dad, scolded her.

Esther looked at the cotton as if she was afraid to touch it. She moved her hands in slow motion. Perhaps her mind was playing tricks on her. She had seen *a few worms*, and she thought there were others on her row. No matter how many times Dad whipped her; she just could not please him. Dad was unreasonable. When Mother spoke up, he became furious. Perhaps Esther's attention span was short, but she was just a child! Moreover, not all children perform on the same level. They will do childish things. Now I recall what Paul expressed in his first letter to the Corinthians.

He wrote, *"When I was a child, I spoke as a child, I understood as a child, I thought as a child: but when I became a man, I put away childish things."*

I Corinthians 13:11 *(KJV)*

The child was simply reacting as a child. She had not come into full knowledge that picking cotton was a *job*. Ruth and I watched Esther receive many lashes. We did not dare speak anything to Dad in her defense. He was subject to turn on us. We knew that action caused a reaction. We had heard Dad shout at Mother after she tried to reason with him. Ruth helped Esther out of concern many times by putting cotton into her sack. Sometimes Esther still got a whipping. She will probably describe them as beatings. I will certainly agree with her.

Dad whipped her until she wet her clothes. Then he said, *"This baby picks mo' cotton than you."* Dad expected me to rise to the challenge, even though I was the baby. As little, and as young as I was, I heard that statement and I knew what it meant. I went to work. I was very eager to learn to do whatever task assigned to me. It was not a fact that I liked picking cotton. The truth of the matter is, I did not want to be whipped and I was afraid too! Our dad made the decision that we were going to pick cotton. Strangely, I was younger than five years old, not much more than a baby was. I should not have been in anybody's cotton field. My parents should have left me with a responsible caretaker.

To my siblings

Let me share more astounding information from the storehouse. Mother did not stand a chance to make a decision, or she did not think she could.

Frankly, she was afraid of Dad because *he was very controlling*. He had a rapacious desire for money, and he was bossy to the point of becoming belligerent. Dad beat Mother many times right before our eyes. We were helpless young children and those were frightening experiences, which we could never forget. We could not erase them from memory if we tried, because they always came back to haunt us. Bad experiences are the hardest ones to forget. Children need counseling after traumatic encounters and sometimes they have problems trusting people.

Those experiences were likening to *rain and windstorms*, which tossed us around before they beat us down. All of us survived and we learned to get up on our feet and press forward. Even though Mother was battered, she kept the faith that we would overcome. We kept working like *Hebrew Slaves*. We noticed some parents carried their babies to the cotton fields and placed them in cardboard boxes. Parents checked on their infants and kept them within close range. That was determination or plain greed. Moreover, "*plantation owners*" required the residents to work. They were not concerned about what was convenient for the workers. There seemed to have been several pharaohs during those times.

Dad bragged to other people after we picked about a *bale* of cotton. His audacity was awesome! He did not seem to be appreciative because he never gave us as much as a hug. He could have told us that we did a good job, *but he did not*. One day he carried me with him to a little convenient store and that was unusual.

"I'll buy you some ice-cream," Dad said to me.
"Ok, ok," I replied in a joyful manner.
I was all excited. I could hardly wait, and my imagination was running wild! I was thinking about the crunchy, tasty cone, and the vanilla flavor. That is um-um-good. We did not have ice cream often. Suddenly, Dad hit his brakes while in route to the store. I was thrown forward and I hit my head on the dashboard. Then I began to cry. Well, I was just a child and there were no seat belts in cars at that time. Dad made a big fuss as if it was my fault. He gave me a mean look and his tone of voice was scary.

"Sit your behind back on the seat," He shouted to me.
"Oh, oh, oh," I cried.
I was sitting back on the seat from the beginning of the trip. I cried even harder after that statement. Tears were running down my face and

they met under my chin. My head was hurting and Dad continued to fuss. He reacted to what could be likening to a *gusty windstorm*, which hit me hard and left me battling to regain my composure. In the meantime, he just starred at me and fussed. It was definitely a mean time. He should not have fussed at me. When we arrived at the store, I do not remember if Dad bought the ice cream, which he had promised me. We returned home and I was too frightened to mention what happened.

One day while stuffing my little sack with cotton, I had a sudden urge to relieve myself. I went to the opposite end of the field. There were no workers in that area and there were no portable toilets in the cotton fields. The owners were not concerned about our needs, so they did not make things convenient for us. We were just manual laborers. I could not find my way back to where my parents were, after I had taken care of business. The cotton was taller than I was and I lost my directions. Therefore, I ended up on another plantation. I knew I had been walking for a long time and finally I realized that I was *lost*. That is when I panicked! I was a horrified little girl who did not know which way to go. I do not remember screaming, but I do remember crying. Luckily, someone found me. Thank God for that person. Things could have been much worse. Mother was worried because she did not know where I had gone. I cannot say Dad was worried but he missed me from helping to fill his cotton sack. I had a pillow case sack. Dad emptied my cotton into his long sack. He may have complained that I caused him to divert his attention from picking cotton for a while. Earning money was his main concern. He *really* had a rapacious desire for money, money and more money. We must have earned plenty *at that time*, but our dad did not put it to good use. We did not have a good supply of clothing; neither did we have an adequate supply of food at all times. I am sure that many others were in the same predicament. Most times, you are not alone.

Reflecting on Cotton

It is the most important fiber that man uses for making clothing. We picked enough cotton to make many, many garments. Those who were in the business should have been happy and very prosperous. Cotton fiber is useful to make many products. Take cotton diapers for instance. They were in demand however; they are almost a thing of the past now. Cotton underwear is very comfortable for wear year-round and especially in the summer. For several years, our dad seemed to think the world would not still exist without the cotton we had to pick. At least that is the way it seems. Millions of Americans depend on cotton for at least part of their livelihood. It was called *king cotton* by our ancestors. We noticed different kinds of cotton. They resembled each other in most ways, but they differed in color of flowers and time of blooming. We picked a lot of cotton, and many have enjoyed the finer things in life as the *result.*

The most harmful insect pests included the boll weevil, bollworm and pink bollworm. Powerful dust or liquid insecticides controlled all these pests except the pink bollworm. The farmer used the poisons that killed the insects, which attacked his plants. Airplanes or machines on the ground applied the insecticides in a fine, mist-like spray or powdery dust that drifted onto all parts of the cotton plant. We observed *airplanes* as they flew over the cotton fields.

Esther can attest that the bollworm was a pest. Had it not been for it, perhaps she would have escaped many lashes. She was reluctant to gather the fluffy snowballs of cotton because of the bollworm. Esther was so afraid and aggravated by the worms that sometimes she picked *one lock of cotton at a time.* That did not work with Pharaoh. Dad expected Esther to grab all the locks of cotton and keep her hands moving. In other words, perform as if she were swimming the Mississippi River. She was battling a storm of *pressure*, which she just could not win. The tension was too great. Esther was so little and sickly, but Dad ignored how frail she was. His mind was set on dollars.

It is a known fact that slaves toiled in the cotton fields of many plantations. They cultivated and picked cotton. The workers received a small salary, but the owners received much profit. That was oppression. The rich has always been connected and the poor has always been disconnected. We were overworked and underpaid. That is how many plantation owners were able to get ahead. They took advantage of the little people, the *poor.* It seemed to be in their minds that they should control everyone. It is no wonder that many have the finer things in life: large luxurious homes on acres of land, several nice automobiles, many rent houses, businesses, large bank accounts, and the list goes on! Their children have money for college; they are given their own cars at the age of 15 or younger. *Slavery* still exists, but it has been modernized, or updated, or one may say "*given a new twist.*" We should remember that it is written in the book of Deuteronomy, "Thou shall not oppress a hired servant that is poor and needy, whether he be of thy brethren, or of thy strangers that are in thy land within thy gates."

Deuteronomy 24:14 (KJV)

We know Deuteronomy is one of the law books, but we must also be reminded: *Therefore, all things whatsoever ye would that men should do to you, do ye even so to them…*

Matthew 7:12 (KJV)

Mishaps and Search for Answers

Mother cooked bread on top of the stove and made gravy. She served Esther. The girl walked right beside me and spilled gravy on my head. I was sitting on the floor. I wondered if she were a weakling or just plain clumsy. Maybe she was both, but I was glad the gravy was not very hot because there was no doctor nearby, not even close. After all, bread and gravy was a change from cornbread and milk. We were without doubt tired and glad to have bread to eat. I wondered, "Where was Pharaoh while we were sitting on the floor eating the *poor man's supper?*" He was our boss and most times, he was not around to eat with us.

I also wondered why Dad insisted that we work so hard as children. I questioned his actions, or was he angry because of his past. His actions proved that something was not right. I learned that his father died when he was very young. Dad took on responsibilities to help his mother. He is one of three children. I am sure there were many things, which he could have done to assist her. He should not have taken on the duties of an adult man at an early age. However, that was said to be an *African tradition* but a child is a child and not responsible for his own well-being. Parents should train children to perform duties according to their capabilities. Dad's hurt, anger and frustration filtered through his life into the lives of his family.

He did not get a *formal education*. Maybe he did not think we deserved one either. Perhaps he wanted us to work hard, or harder than he did. Surely, he realizes we are not responsible for the way he was brought up. I would like to know did his dad '*beat*' him. I asked myself, "How could he be so unlearned?" Maybe it was a case of, "*like father, like son.*" Apparently, something was not right. That reminded me of other things. I do not recall ever seeing or hearing him pray, and he never went to worship service with us. He accepted Christ when he was a young boy. Those made me wonder, "Why didn't he attend worship service?" I had many questions and never enough answers.

"Where was Dad when we went to church?, I asked Mother.

"Was he somewhere gambling on Sundays?," I continued but she was quiet.

"Baby, I don't know," She finally answered.

"Maybe he was somewhere playing dominos," I said in a low voice.

Chapter 3

Living with Dad Was Hard

Education Sacrificed

Ruth and Esther were school age. They were not permitted to go to school regularly, but Dad allowed them to go on the "*rainy days.*" They could not pick cotton when it was raining. It did not matter to him what our mother said. He had so much *audacity.* One day Esther and I were talking. I asked her, "Do you remember what Dad said about you and Ruth going to school?" I reminded her.

"Use the paper wrapper from the meat that I bought and teach the chullen to *write on it*, Dad said to Mother.

"I remember that, sure thing oh yeah," Esther said as if the words were ringing in her ears.

"Hum, I like his nerves," I replied.

He did not buy very much meat. That meant paper was scarce. Dad was the boss and he abused Mother, and neglected us. It was either his way, or no way. One might say that Dad ruled with an "*iron fist.*" When I look back on the yesteryears, I clearly recall Mother saying that he beat her badly and burst her eardrum. She longed to return home to her parents. She even asked Dad to drive the old model car home, but he refused to do so. Perhaps it was time to hitchhike, but Mother had three children. It was very characteristic of her to be soft spoken and easy-going. She was such a humble person and very passive. In her quiet tone of voice, she said to Dad repeatedly, *"Take me home."* It was no doubt time to have a serious conversation, especially since Dad was so stubborn or rebellious.

Dad was so cruel. He showed no concern for his children and he caused us to be troubled. He did not demonstrate love at home. He even took our mother's money. That was disrespectful of her rights. Dad seemed to think we had no rights. After all, we worked and he took the money and used it as he pleased. It appeared that we were to obey his orders at all times, and we were *not* allowed to make mistakes. Children should be taught to work, but they should not be forced to earn a living for the family rather than get an education. Dad did not set a good example of a father. Scripture says

Train up a child in the *way he should go: and when he is old, he will not depart from it.*

Proverbs 22:6 (KJV)

If parents do not study God's Word, they may not know what it says. If they do not hear God's Word, they cannot make application. It was his mother's responsibility to train him. She was an active member of Saint Paul Baptist Church in her community. That led me to believe she heard the Word and it was her duty to study God's Word for herself.

Dad fathered another child, a daughter. She was born one month before my sister Esther who is four years older than I am. Mother knew about the woman who apparently was a mistress of Dad's, but I did not hear a discussion about his other child. I learned about her years later.

"Do you have a son?," I asked Dad.
"Naw, naw I aint got no son," He replied after hesitating.
I decided to close that conversation.

I recalled on some weekends Dad took our money and went to Mississippi. I was very young, but I heard our mother say that is where he went. Perhaps, he played dominoes, which seemed to have been a favorite game of his. He was a gambler. He also had a mistress there, the nerve of him! After one trip, he returned home and found no food prepared.

"Why didn't you cook?," He asked Mom.

I do not know how she answered him, but that was a rhetorical question. He was much unlearned! He had not purchased any groceries and he had all of the money. Mother did not know when he would return. Dad left us to survive by eating whatever food Mother could provide for us, or starve. It seems as though he did not care. He was a very controlling and self-centered individual. In other words, it was all about what he had to say and what might be accomplished for him. Family matters were not a top priority. Dad was never empathetic and that is one reason why he used excessive force to accomplish his goal. He would have done well to clothe himself with kindness, humbleness of mind, meekness, and longsuffering. I told a family member, "Think about the kind of person who is characterized by good traits, and all of us fall short somewhere!"

Dad hit our mother and my oldest sister tried to defend her. She was just a young girl about eleven years old.
"Daddy don't hit her," Ruth said.
He ignored her.
She said repeatedly, "Daddy don't hit her."
Ruth pleaded with him while my other sister and I sat on the floor with our backs against the wall. Every time there was drama, we sat there and cried while we watched in disbelief. It was traumatic. That type of action may affect one's life in later years. In addition, time after time, something happened to remind me of our dramatic past.

On another occasion, Ruth tried to defend Mother after Dad hit her as if he were a boxing champion. Ruth jumped up and went to Mom's rescue. Dad threw Ruth against the wall

"O' I'm dead, I'm dead," She cried.
Dad never looked around. He continued to fight Mother. Esther and I watched Ruth fall and Esther thought Ruth was actually dying. We were afraid and Esther was always dra-ma-tic! Dad was just cruel! He did not care who he hurt.

Maybe two weeks later, Mother needed dental care. Dad carried her to a dentist who rendered the needed service. After returning home, he struck her on her face. I do not know what Mother may have said to provoke Dad. I stood there in awe, and I cried, "*Daddy no, no daddy!*" I could not stand there and watch him hurt Mom without saying something. I was scared, young, and I could not stop him but I cried out to him. Mom was in pain and he hurt her even more. I cried because I felt her pain! I suppose Dad did not want to pay the price for dental treatments. He was always mean and showed no compassion. That was not love; it was like pouring salt on her wound. He was cruel.

He left home. Maybe he needed to cool off. He went to play dominoes and returned only to boast about how much money he had won, and whom he had beaten up. He seemed to be in the mood to fight. I never saw him pick on anyone his size. Sometimes Dad left home and stayed away a number of days. He was not even concerned about the well-being of his family. Therefore, nothing was new, and we wondered when Dad would come to his senses. He never took time to hold a decent conversation with us, and he never played with us as some dads do. We were looking for love from him. We did not receive it.

Impromptu Visit

Sometime later, Dad went to Mississippi and returned with his mistress. She could neither read nor write her own name. She would not have recognized it if it were written in block letters. She was illiterate. At that time I did not know just how unversed she was. She lived within walking distance from us. Dad had some nerves! He put her right under Mom's nose. Our neighbors were discussing the situation, a modern day soap opera. Enough of anything is enough. Mother saw Dad at his mistress' house and she decided to visit them. She wanted to check things out. Apparently, she wanted to know what was going on, but Dad was not one who was approachable even though he was her husband. The domineering pharaoh was on the premises of his mistress. He put on a grand performance, which was very characteristic of him. He just had to prove a point. After all, his mistress was in town and he wanted to prove his masculinity. I am surprised Mother even inquired about the mysterious woman, even though neighbors were gossiping about the affair. Mom did not know anything about the strange Mississippi woman, but she did know *"mean pharaoh."* He held us captive as if we were Hebrew Slaves and refused to set us free. He would not carry us to Louisiana, but he took time to go to *Mississippi*. He did as he pleased, and we did as he commanded. He was the taskmaster, mean cruel dad. His rule was no one challenges the taskmaster.

Outcome of the visit

Dad beat Mom with a water hose, which is a flexible tube for conveying a liquid. She returned home crying. There were blue and purple bruises on her body from the lashes with the hose. She suffered through a monstrous storm of *inflictions*. Dad thought the battle was over.

Most of us have heard that *"we reap what we sow"* and "what goes around comes around." Well, sometimes when our crops come up we do not like them, but that is what we planted. Most times, we plant a few seeds and many plants are produced. We may not like the results of our actions, but we must deal with them.

After a little while, there was a change. We do know that a change will come. Well, Pharaoh became ill. Our mother was beaten often, battered, and bruised. She was the *Good Samaritan* woman who rescued him. She informed the property owner who summoned an ambulance. Well, well, had it not been for Mom's quick action, Dad just might have died. Maybe one would liken him to a feline, which is said to have *nine lives*. Anyway, he was carried to a hospital where he underwent an operation to remove his appendix, an appendectomy. I recall the big black, strange-looking automobile pulled up in front of the house, which was called home. It appeared to be or resembled a hearse. I did not want my mom to get inside it, and I was frightened when they put Dad on the stretcher. I did not know what to think, but I wondered if he were dying. He was such a mean man, probably too mean to die. Anyway, Mom went to the hospital with him. I kept thinking of her. She was so modest, but Dad was cold hearted, a pharaoh.

Soon after his illness, Pharaoh was himself again. He had forgotten or just brushed aside the fact that Mother was by his side when he was helpless. She was there to lend a helping hand, to render whatever service, to see him through the whole ordeal.

"God will deal with him in His own time," She said in a mild tone.

One might think Dad would have changed or become a better person after his illness. No, no, he was still hard-hearted. He is likened unto Pharaoh in the book of Exodus who would not let the Israelites go free. Even after the ten plagues, Pharaoh was still hard-hearted. After I pondered Dad's behavior, I reminded myself that no one is perfect. All of us have ways, which we need to amend, but we must first recognize that we are wrong. It is a good thing to go to God in prayer as David did.

Search me, O God, and know my heart: try me, and know my thoughts and see if there be any wicked way in me, and lead me in the way everlasting.

Psalm 139:23-24(KJV)

God gives us a chance and another chance. Dad is truly blessed. He has lived beyond four score and seven years. God stands at the door of one's heart and knocks. If Dad will open up, God will come in. He is willing and able to make him clean inside. He will also give him joy, peace and love. God is not the author of confusion. He is love. However, Satan is the father of all lies. Confusion usually starts with a lie.

If one is blind, God can open his eyes and he will behold His beauty. Not all blind men are physically blind, but they have refused to see the light. They have called right wrong and wrong right. As I recall, "*There is a way which seemeth right unto a man; but the end thereof are the ways of death.*"

God is the same today as He was yesterday, and tomorrow He will not change. He has worked many miracles, and He is still in the healing business!

If Dad would open up, acknowledge God, and be transformed by the renewing of his mind, God will come in. Dad will be changed from the creature that he is. Nothing is too hard for God!

I call to remembrance the prayer of Elisha.
And Elisha prayed, and said, Lord, I pray thee, open his eyes, that he may see.

II Kings 6:17 (KJV)

Chapter 4

A Trip to the Hospital

Unfortunate Act

One summer day, I found a coin while playing outside. I thought it was money, a quarter or two bits. That is the way my grandparents described a quarter. I was so excited I ran straightaway and told my big sister. After she observed it, she proclaimed that it was just a washer. That is a flat ring of metal, which can be utilized to give tightness to a joint. I was highly disappointed. She tried to remove it from my little hand but I held it tightly. I was determined to hold on to it. Ruth was larger and naturally stronger than I was. After struggling for a while, she managed to succeed. She removed it and threw it away. I was watching so closely, I saw where it landed. I retrieved it and again she struggled to regain control, but to no avail. Without thinking, I put the object into my mouth. Ruth thought if she tickled me, she could remove it, but not so. I swallowed, *"gulp"* and it was gone. With the object out of reach for me and for her too, we were helpless. I could not speak one word. As I recall, my chest felt heavy. Immediately, Ruth knew that I was in trouble. I swallowed the washer. She panicked and ran to locate our mom to tell her what happened. Thank God, Mom was not very far away. Dad could not be found. I do not know if Mother tried to dislodge the object from my throat. I was dazed and could not say a word. That time it was I who desperately needed medical attention. I had been bad. I was mischievous, and the result was not good.

Mom's Faith

There was no ambulance service for me. I never knew the reason but I do know Mother left home walking with me on her shoulder. No one was available with an automobile. Mom was in route to the hospital, which I am sure was miles away. This is something to look at metaphorically. A storm of *"trouble-at-hand"* arose. It was a violent, atmospheric upheaval. Mom and I were in a little ship at sea. The small vessel began to rock and rill like a drunken man, and the cargo came close to being lost. The ship was struggling to move forward, but the force of strong wind slowed its pace. The anchor was in place and it gripped the solid rock. In spite of the storm, the little ship kept striving to reach its destination because there was still hope. Mom sent out an S.O.S. The ship of *"deliverance"* was definitely in trouble. The distress call went to the master, who is the captain (*Jesus*). He is the **"Savior of Souls."** Mom knew He was able to speak to the storm and the wind and rain would obey His voice.

The voice of the Lord is upon the waters: the God of glory thundered: the Lord is upon many waters. The voice of the Lord is powerful; the voice of the Lord is full of majesty.

Psalm 29: 3-4 (KJV)

In Reality

Mom was likened unto Eunice, the mother of Timothy. She had unfeigned faith. She held on and continued to travel because she knew she was going through the storm. It was not time to stop or to slow her pace by choice. I am sure her little bundle of joy was a bit heavy, and Mother's heart was equally heavy. She did what any mother would have done. I was in trouble and she was determined to get help. As she traveled that long road, without doubt she was talking to her master, the Sustainer of life. Perhaps there was very little traffic on the road at that time. It was about midday and the sun was high in the sky, yet it appeared to be *dark and near midnight*. When trouble comes, it always appears to be dark. Mom desperately needed a ride to reach the nearest medical facility. I know she spoke to the "rock of her salvation." She called "Jesus, I need you right now Lord to make a way for me." I perceive that God stepped in right on time. He is never late but on time, in time, every time. It had not been long since she laid one child to rest and suddenly another *"storm of intense sadness"* in her life. Nevertheless, God gave Mom strength. No matter what the price, no matter how rough and rugged the road, nor how strongly the wind blew, she was determine to get help. Mother kept praying. Then the wind changed in directions and its force drove her. She kept traveling and she knew in whom to put her trust. Mom often read her Bible and recalled the teachings of Solomon.

Trust in the Lord with all thine heart; and lean not unto thine own understanding.

Proverbs 3:5 (KJV)

The Miracle

As I formed a mental image of Mom, she kept traveling with her companions, *"grace"* and *"mercy."* Each step brought her closer and closer to our destination. Although there were still curves in her pathway and hills to climb, she kept pressing on. Mother struggled with me on her shoulder as she looked ahead through tear-stained eyes and observed a star of hope. I can imagine she was very tired, weary, and worn, but faith always sees a star of hope! I do not know when we arrived at the hospital but I am appreciative for Mom. We arrived. I do not recall the name of the health care facility but Emmanuel, God was with us. A doctor removed the washer. I never understood the position of the object but maybe it was lodged in the area of my trachea. That was a dangerous location, and I thank God that my airway was not completely obstructed. I can imagine had Mom stumbled one time, I could have been gone, but God saved me. Perhaps the washer had a hole in the center. If so, it provided a passageway for breathing. God kept me for a reason or many reasons. Thank you Lord! God is awesomeness. How great thou art!

Words were inadequate to verbalize my gratefulness to Mom who had great determination, and my big sister who reacted quickly under pressure. I thank God for physicians who have attained knowledge and skills to perform such tasks. I was a child and knew nothing about doctors. Nevertheless, within a short period I was able to ingest nourishment and returned home shortly thereafter. With Mother by my side, I was confident that everything was all right. Children always feel better when their moms are caring for them. Others may be qualified to do the job, but no one can take the place of Mom. I remember Dad said, "You cost me a lot of money." Then I wondered what was important to him. Moncy is all I could imagine! Mother was not pleased with my actions, but she did not rant or rave about them. She was concerned about my life! Repeatedly, Dad informed someone of what happened. He said I caused him to spend a lot of money. He should have been thankful to God that matters were not worse. Instead, he was concerned about a few scanty dollars. I had worked like a grown-up picking cotton to fill his sack while he boasted about it.

"We made mo' money than everybody else," He bragged.
"What did he do with it?," We wondered.

Money was his main concern. When he had it, he did not do the right thing with it. His priorities were backwards however, no one dared to tell him so.

Chapter 5

My Big Sister

Chore Time

I was very much dependent upon Ruth like a crutch. In other words, she was like second mom in a way. She took care of me when Mom was not at home. One-day big sister fell from a window, and I screamed as if she were dead. I was shaking from fear. I was just a little girl and I did not know what to do to assist her. Esther was right there, but she was scared as usual. I guess she was a *scary cat*! Even she did not know what to do. Dad had whipped her so much, maybe she could not think instantly. Because of the fall, Ruth had bruises on one of her arms. That was enough to frighten any child. A bruise is bluish on the skin. It is an injury, which is caused by striking or pressing without breaking the skin, causing a subcutaneous hemorrhage. After a few days, the signs of injury had vanished and Ruth was ready to resume her duties.

We transported drinking water in pails from a pump, which was a short distance away. A pail of water was always reserved and left beside the pump. The next time we returned to pump water; we used the pail of reserved water to prime the pump. We did that by pouring water into it, raising, and lowering the handle several times. We could feel the pressure of drawing water each time the process was repeated. The first water from the pump was not always clear. It was allowed to flow freely a few minutes.

As it flowed, it became clearer and clearer. That meant it was good for human consumption. Contaminates or impurities were removed. There are only two sources from which to obtain water. They are #1: rivers and lakes or from #2: the ground. I always wanted to help my sisters with the chore of transporting water. My pail was a little syrup bucket. After all the pails were filled to their brims, we were ready to travel. We made our way down the little well traveled dusty trail, which had been made for a shorter route. We started out very energetic but after walking a few minutes my *"wee"* pail seemed to be too heavy! Suddenly, I wanted to be carried.

"Totey me Ruth, totey me," I cried.

Big sister lowered her pail to the ground, picked me up, and placed me on her hip. She picked up her pail of water and started out again. Esther carried her pail and my "wee" bucket. Most likely, that was a struggle for her.

Although we had to pump our own water, we were blessed among millions. I am reminded that some people in other countries would treasure the opportunity to collect clean drinking water. Some bathe in the rivers and lakes, and collect drinking water from the same source without a form of purification. Sometimes we think we are barely surviving until we witness others who are struggling more than we are. We must be grateful and thank God. It is of the Lord's mercies that we are not consumed and His compassions fail not.

Mom's Remedy

When it was time to retire for the night Ruth carried cornbread or whatever bread we had left over to bed for me. It was placed inside an old pocketbook. That was done in order to avoid getting out of bed to get bread for me when I asked for it. Perhaps I dropped breadcrumbs on the bed, but I do not recall any complaints. I was the baby and I slept between my two sisters.

Many days and nights, it was very cold in Arkansas and the butane gas was low or in short supply. On one morning as I recall, I pulled my chair up close to the heater while trying to get warm. I burned my left knee. The heater apparently was very hot, as I remember; my knee had a bubbly sore on it. Mother did not have silvadene cream to apply to the wound. It was unheard of, but she used the old remedy: *baking soda mixed with syrup*. It was applied as a salve and the wound healed gradually without infection. The scar remained and it is very noticeable today. I thank Jehovah God and I thank my caring mother who believed not so much in the remedy but in God. Mom had faith that her Heavenly Father would work a miracle. He did, and that was a blessing. My maternal grandmother, Dolly also used old remedies. We were told our ancestors believed strongly in the use of many remedies for illnesses. As I think along the line of healing, I recall a passage of scripture, which points out spiritual gifts. One of those gifts is the gift of healing. The Spirit gives all of the gifts and we know that all good gifts come from God. How good God is!

We did not get medical care from professionals unless it was an emergency, life or death. Big sister was always close by to help me during the absence of Mom. Esther was always there too, but she seldom offered assistance.

Alternative for Heat

It was very, very cold in Wilson, Arkansas during the winter. There was lots of snow. We never seemed to have enough blankets or quilts for cover. The alternative was to use old clothes, coats, or whatever was available to keep us warm .I told Rachel how Mother heated the *smoothing irons* by placing them on the heater. She wrapped them up and placed them in the bed to warm our feet. How sad that was but we survived! That was the objective. Mom was definitely a survivor. One winter morning the snow was deep. Mother was at work, Dad was not home either. My big sister decided that was the perfect time to bury Dad's shotgun. It was not a bad idea. She was thinking survival! After all, Dad had threatened to kill all of us. We breathed a sigh of relief after the gun was buried.

As time passed, it was another season. We were home when a truck arrived. It was loaded to capacity with manual laborers. They had come to pick cotton. Progress had been made and a water pump was in our own *front yard*. A woman got off the truck and walked toward the pump to get a drink of water. Esther who was always scared, decided to be *"bossy."* Maybe she was growing up and making changes.

"Don't put your mouth on that pump!," She yelled to the stranger.

The stranger paid no attention to her command but continued to do just what she had started. She came to the door after she had apparently quenched her thirst. We ran like mice scrambling for safety from the intruder. Esther who had been bossy thought she had bolted the door shut. In the rush, she no doubt *missed the connection.* The woman walked right inside. Esther hid behind another door. I was always with my big sister. She crawled underneath one of the beds and I followed her, but to my surprise, the woman saw my *foot* and attempted to pull me out from our *so-called hiding place.*

"O-h, O-h!," I screamed.

Big sister did not say a word. She was silent as if the cat had her tongue. That is what we said when one would not speak, especially when spoken to. She held me tightly. I was depending on her for *protection.* The stranger released my foot and left the house after a few minutes. We were afraid to come out from what we thought was a good "*hiding place.*" Esther had gotten us into that predicament, and she was the first one to come out.

"Y'all can come out now!," She made the announcement.

In other words, *all was clear.* Esther did not dare do that again: try to bluff someone. I am not sure of the reason why we were home on that particular day. We got into trouble a number of times. We played on the bed as some children do today. In the late forties and early fifties, we used the old cotton stir-mattresses with coiled bedsprings. The three of us jumped up and down as if we were on a springboard. We had a good time! That was entertainment for us. We knew better but we did it because it was fun and we were home alone! I remembered saying, "When the cat is away the mouse will play."

There were many people in the area. Some of them were Mexicans. Perhaps they spoke very fluent Spanish, but I was unable to comprehend it. It was a language, which, I had not heard until we moved to Arkansas. Neither was I accustomed to being in the presence of other ethnic groups.

Another episode

Dad had an old model Ford. We were at home alone again and chose to play in the car. Big sister opened the door. For some unknown reason, I placed my little left finger into the hinge of the door. Ruth slammed the door shut and it cut my finger. The first joint seemed to be almost severed. It appeared to be hanging and dangling by the skin. I screamed and screamed for help, *"O-h."* I was in excruciating pain. I saw blood streaming down my hand. That was enough to scare me. Big sister panicked as she had done before. She went to get our mother who came quickly and bandaged my finger up. She did not have a first aid kit as one may have today. She had the *"common sense"* kit. That meant a lot more than anything did. I do not know what her remedy was that time. Surely, she touched my little hand with care and concern. Mom poured on much love and wrapped faith and hope around my finger. She believed it would knit back together and be whole again. We did not get the chance to play in the car. We forgot we ever attempted to do so after all the excitement. Thank God, my finger healed without treatment by a physician. My fingernail came off several times but I never worried about it. That was a reminder of what happened. I still have my whole finger and I thank God!

Outsider

One evening Mom was asked to baby sit for her property owner. She did not dare refuse. Mrs. Hadnott left her son, Jack at our house. He was a naughty little *"white boy,"* who wanted to have his way. He hit me on my head with a broomstick. He deserved a whipping, but Mom just put him in bed. If she had hit Jack on his derriere, I am positive he would have told his mom. He would have given her the impression that my mom beat him. The *"rascal"* put a knot on my head. That little brat left his mark on me.

Jack had chewing gum in his mouth. He threw it across the room.

"Git it Ruth, git it," He said.

I do not know if Ruth ever found the gum because the room was dark. The next morning I woke up and Jack was gone. My remark was, *"good riddance."*

Chapter 6

A Trip to Louisiana

Train Ride

I recall the manifold episodes, which occurred during early childhood. One captured undivided attention. My beloved mother's parents lived in the state of Louisiana. They were Willie and Dolly Salters-Clarkson. Both were off springs of large families. Mother kept in touch with her parents by writing letters while we were away from home. Of course, it was the only way. We had no telephone service although Alexander Graham Bell invented the system for transmission of sound or speech to a distant point long before my grandparents were born. We were lacking in power to obtain a telephone even in 1949 because we were extremely poor. Our family was struggling to survive. We could not afford such a luxury. We were quite a distance from being well connected. Of course, that was not geographically, but financially.

Mother decided to visit with her parents. I do not recall any distinct circumstances, which prompted the visit. However, I think just being away from home was reason enough. Surely, she longed to be with her parents because at home there was love. A mother loves her children all the time and she shows it in many ways. I must admit there are some odd mothers who neglect their children, and I hope that will change. Some fathers love their children too, although many have strange ways of showing it. In addition, some do not make it know at all. Children want to hear their parents say, "*I love you.*" More importantly, they want to feel loved.

Mother had three children at that time and I was the youngest. I am the fourth child because her second child died. Therefore, I had the opportunity to travel with her. We traveled by train and it was an interesting and most exciting trip. I cannot explain how emotionally stirred I was. As I allow my mind to travel back in time, I envision myself sitting closely beside my mother. I was definitely a mama's baby, but considering all the facts, I had no other choice. Everything within my view brought exhilaration as I looked out the window of the moving train. I was delighted and I am certain my little face was aglow. I do not even remember carrying cornbread in a pocketbook.

The Reunion

Upon arrival at my maternal grandparents' house, I was still excited and they were so happy to see us. As I recall the reunion, there was an abundant supply of food. That was unheard of at our house in Wilson, Arkansas. My grandfather started a fire in the fireplace with a large backlog and little logs in the front. He used kindling, small strips of a board to get the fire started. He also piled on chips of wood. We sat around the fireplace and talked. Within minutes, the fire was blazing and soon the room was fairly warm. Grandma, Mom and Cousin Ella D. were there. I noticed everyone sat closely to the fire and I saw darks spots on each one's legs.

"What's wrong with you'll legs," I asked.
"They were burned by the fire," Mom responded.
"They not sore," She continued.
I did not understand that. Now I know why. All of them pulled their chairs close to the fire so they would be warm. When they felt too warm they pushed their chairs back, but then they were cold again. Therefore, they pulled their chairs up close to the fire and refused to push them back. Surely, there was a solution: *cover their legs with an apron.* That is my thought today. I was a child then and I would not have known to suggest it. We live and we learn but Grandma wore an apron everyday. I wonder why she allowed the fire to burn her legs. Surely, they could have done something to protect their legs. Cousin Ella D. was younger than Grandma was.

"Why didn't they have a remedy to shield their legs from the heat?," I wondered.

Ashes accumulated in the fireplace as the logs burned. Grandpa roasted sweet potatoes under the hot ashes. As the wood burned, he put more ashes and fire coals over the potatoes. Occasionally he checked them to determine if they were soft. Soon they were removed, and he brushed the ashes away. We peeled them as we ate and boy, oh boy they were good!

My grandparents did not have a heating furnace, which was invented by *Alice Parker*. They were not that fortunate nevertheless; we thanked God for such as we had. It was a joy to just recline beside the fireplace and watch the wood logs burn. Surely, Mother had plenty to discuss. She was home with her mom and all mothers give advice to their children. The atmosphere was so different and everyone was calm! I was completely comfortable and not the least bit afraid. No one abused us in any way. I am sure Mother discussed the possibility of returning home to live, but Dad was so cruel and "*money hungry.*" He was a pharaoh!

Grandma pieced quilts from scraps of fabric. She used old clothes too. It was a common practice for women in those days. At least four women gathered at one house to finish the project after the quilt was pieced together. As I recall, cotton was placed between the colorful top and the plain bottom, which was made from cotton sacks. Somehow, the quilt was attached to two narrow boards, which were about a foot longer than the quilt. A long cord or rope was attached to each corner of the boards. Some type of hooks was in the ceiling to hang the quilt up. When the group was ready to work, they gathered their heavy thread, needles, thimbles, and scissors before taking their places to begin quilting. They pulled their wooden chairs up for comfort and began the quilting process. They saved all the empty thread spools. They raised the quilt nearly to the ceiling and retired for the day after working several hours. They returned the next day and resumed their work. Sometimes the four worked during the night. They finish the quilt by rolling the edge of the bottom piece over the top about two inches. Then they whip stitched the roll. The finished project was colorful and beautiful.

Grandfather's Job

My grandfather owned an ax and a saw for cutting wood. He cut short pieces of wood to be used in the old black kitchen stove for cooking and longer pieces of wood for the fireplace. The wood chips were used to help start a fire. He owned a handsaw and a long saw, which had two handles. Two people utilized it by working together. Grandfather was a good provider. He ensured that we had plenty of wood. When the supply was getting low, he used two mules and a wagon to go to the forest. He cut the wood, loaded the wagon, returned home, and unloaded the wood all by himself. That was a task but one in which he handled very well. Grandpa said the overseer allowed one of the men on the plantation to use a tractor many times to bring a whole tree to his house for wood burning. He cut wood from that tree, as he needed it. There were times when he cut enough wood to last several days. During the winter, he cut wood and placed it on the front porch.

Grandpa

Return to Arkansas

We enjoyed our short visit, which ended too soon. We returned to Arkansas. I am not sure who took care of my two sisters during our absence. Perhaps that was a deciding factor to return home as soon as we did. Mom and I enjoyed the trip and we had a story to tell the girls. Ruth and Esther were fine. They had no unusual experiences or terrible reports. Thank God for our safe return!

Chapter 7

Baby Sister #5

Trouble Ahead

On May 5, 1950 Mother did not work. She was at home in bed. Time was nearing for delivery of her next child. We sat in our usual position on the floor with our backs against the wall. We were told to be quiet and stay away from the action. The midwife was there to perform her duties. That was serious business. We sat quietly and waited for the news. After a while, we heard a little one cry, a baby girl. She made her entrance and another chapter was written in Mom's life. Baby sister #5 was greeted. I was five years old at that time and had no idea what was in store for me, a task indeed.

Mother was fine and after a few months, she resumed her usual duties. She left me to baby sit. I was not much older than a toddler was, but I was attending to a baby. I had no knowledge of babysitting. Several bottles of milk were prepared and left conveniently for feeding the little one. First day on the job, as soon as the baby woke up I gave her a bottle of milk. I would have given her more but she would not take it. Oh! I did not want her to cry because I was home alone, and I was afraid. I do not recall any instructions to burp the baby after each feeding. I overfed the little girl. Actually, I did it inadvertently. Mom should have left us in the care of a responsible adult. Nevertheless, I can say the boss made that decision just as he made all the others. As I look back down the rough road, which was filled with multiple obstacles, I immediately hear the harsh commands, which rolled from his lips. He was the dominant force in our lives.

I recall standing on the side of the road with my little right fist clinched and my thumb turned up. That was the sign to use when thumbing a ride. Only I did not want to ride anywhere. I was trying to get someone's attention. I was expecting someone to stop so that I could send a message to the overseer. I was a child and I did not know any better than to try such. Some man stopped to listen to me.

"What's the matter," He asked.
"Ring the bell so my mom and Dad will know it's time to come home," I said.
"Oh, I can't do that," The man said.
I walked back inside the house with tears in my eyes. I was very disappointed and the day seemed to be so very, very long.

Dad sent Ruth or Esther home to observe, give instructions to me, and ensure that all was well with us. Esther was nine years old. Ruth was eleven. One may conclude that Ruth should have been at home with all of us although it was not her responsibility. It would have made a tremendous difference, and little Anna would have been most appreciative. One day Esther came home and found the baby crying frantically. She had been awake for quite some time. Apparently, something was wrong. Esther grabbed the paregoric, a soothing medicine.

"This will make her sleep," She said to me.

Esther gave Anna a dose of the medicine. Then she walked away and left me holding the baby. I thought she had put the medicine away properly. She left the house and I looked up, saw the bottle, and cap on the table. I knew that was not going to work. Esther forgot to recap the bottle of medication *before she left the house*. Perhaps her attention span was short or maybe she was distracted.

I hurried to the door.
"Esther, Es-ther," I called out desperately.

She kept walking in a hurry. She could not hear me. Maybe Dad told her to be back to the cotton field within so many minutes.

"Don't touch no medicine, and don't give the baby nothing but her milk," I had been instructed by Dad in a harsh manner.

I recalled the instructions. I did as I was told and I did not dare touch the paregoric, not even to recap it. I stood there wondering what to do. I reminded myself, "I tried unsuccessfully to call Esther, but she could not hear me." I simply left the bottle uncapped for fear of the result. As I think about it today, I could have recapped the bottle and Dad would have never known that Esther left it open. However, he had a way of traumatizing us. When mean cruel Dad returned home from work he made a big fuss after he saw the medicine on the table.

"Git out yo' clothes." Said Dad.
"Daddy I didn't do it, I didn't," I said, begging him not to whip me.
I backed up all the way against the wall while crying. Dad put the hurt on me. He would not listen to me and Esther would not explain that she had left the paregoric on the table. Maybe she did not realize what she had done. Dad was a pharaoh and very unreasonable. He beat me unmercifully. I swore to him that I did not do anything wrong. That was one time I wished that I had done what I was told not to do. Had I recapped the medicine, maybe I would have avoided the beating. That is hindsight!

Misconduct

I carefully considered the fact that I received a beating, which I did not deserve. I asked myself, "Why leave a five year old child alone to attend to a baby?" I view that as a prime example of ignorance. Child protection services will have a field day with anyone who does such. That is, if they are aware of it.

As I observe people, it is obvious that some never grow up. They are satisfied with the way they conduct themselves, and no one can persuade them to do otherwise. Some have convinced themselves that what they do is right and others are wrong. May God have mercy on us. His mercies are new every morning and everyday is an opportunity to do better.

Now I can identify with those who were falsely accused. I sympathize with those who were thrown into prison for crimes, which they did not commit. They paid the price, suffered unjustly, and some died because of decisions, which unbelievers made. Many cries for mercy *have not* been acknowledged, and those with the power to free them by speaking the truth opened not their mouths. Neither did Esther speak out. She let me take a beating for her mistake. Perhaps, she was fearful because she had received many lashes from Pharaoh's whip. I did not understand then, but thank God for knowledge and understanding, which came as time went by. Solomon wrote, *"In all thy getting, get understanding."*

Pharaoh was not concerned about the baby. I gave the decision in-depth thought. He was scrambling for money. That is why I was home alone with the infant! Just a few weeks later, Anna was in Mother's bed and suddenly out of anger, Dad snatched the blanket from underneath her. At that moment, she fell to the floor. Dad went all the way left, exploded like a bomb! He and Mom were in the middle of an altercation about money and little innocent Anna was hurt. Mother was only trying to hold on to a few dollars, which were rightfully hers. She often placed her money underneath her pillow. That really was no place to hide it, but it was accessible for her. Truly, no one should fear loosing his or her money to their spouse in their own house, or anywhere. There was no reason to beat Mother or hurt anyone. I remember the incident clearly. Pharaoh was very cruel. No one had beaten him for his actions or wrong doings. Mother was afraid of him and she knew she could not overpower him, but many women would have found a way to deal with him. Perhaps Mother was thinking of a statement, which was made by several who knew him. Word was out that Dad and a relative had done something horrible. That alone was frightening!

Scary Moment

Again, I was home alone with baby sister, Anna. The house was fairly dark and I was a bit frightened. I thought I saw the shadow of someone else in the house. Perhaps my imagination was playing tricks on me. Fear had set in and the least noise scared me. I heard that some houses have ghosts in them. Well, the house was old and I wondered if anyone had died there. I was more comfortable sitting or standing on the porch. Older people used the word garret instead. Therefore, I picked the baby up, put her into my little arms, and went outside. While standing there I began to shake her. All of a sudden, I dropped the little girl and she fell to the ground on the little brick walkway. Thank God, the porch was not high off the ground. I grabbed the baby up.

"Oh no, oh no, oh no!, I cried."
I was afraid she was hurt because she really screamed. Nothing seemed to be wrong with her lungs. Surely, she has a healthy pair. She cried and cried for a while. When Mother came home, I did not dare tell her about the incident for fear of getting another beating. Since there were no scratches or bruises on the little girl I thought, "I might be out of danger." Mom did not ask any questions and I did not volunteer any information. I had learned another lesson, when to speak and when to keep quiet.

"He that would live in peace and at ease should not speak all that he knows, nor judge all that he sees."

—Author unknown

Chapter 8

Return to Louisiana

In 1951, Mother packed our belongings *several times* in anticipation of returning home. Each time Pharaoh *changed his mind*. Finally, one day we were all packed and ready to travel. We did not have Samsonite Luggage but the bed sheets served the purpose. We were definitely overjoyed. At last, Dad was ready to drive the old vehicle in route to Louisiana. It was a long ride to our grandparents' house but we were on our way. Perhaps it just appeared to be a long ride. We had longed to see that day many times. Dad stopped to buy something from a store. Mother bought some candy. She gave Esther a *mound bar* and shortly after she had eaten the candy she said, "My stomach hurts." She was just a *delicate child!* When we reached our destination, we were relieved. I do not recall Esther complaining about her stomach problem. Maybe it was a case of bad nerves.

Dad returned to Arkansas. After all, he had a mistress there. However, he could not stand the thought of his family living in Louisiana without him. He could not boss us around, and he was no longer the "*task-master.*" Therefore, he relocated in Shreveport, Louisiana. Of course, he carried his mistress with him even though she could not read or write. Apparently, that was not a problem. Maybe he was in love. It hides a multitude of faults.

We lived in Grand Bayou, Louisiana with my mother's parents. They were elated to have us at home. We were happy to be close to other family members especially our first cousins, the Taylors, and Clarksons. We were one big happy family. Sometimes we slept on a quilt on the floor and it was not a problem. We were accustomed to it. The difference being, we were jubilant! Sometimes we talked until midnight. It was all fun and games. It was very relaxing to lie on the front porch while the grown-ups were visiting at night. Of course, that was during the summer. When people are happy, it does not matter if they sleep on the floor, or sit on the floor. They might even put their plate of food on the floor. It works out fine! I have been there.

The conversations of the grown-ups were interesting and sometimes awesome. They talked about the happenings of slavery and etcetera.

"I hid under a bridge to keep slave owners from taking me," Grandpa said.
My mother and her sister informed us about the flood of 1945. There was a levee near Red River but apparently, it did not prevent the flood.

"During the high water, we put things in bags and hung them from the ceiling," Mom said.
"I was living with Mama and Papa when I was carried from the house in a boat," Auntie said to us, while holding her hands.
"Somebody brought me to town and I stayed with Aunt Matt until it was time to go to the Charity Hospital. That's where I gave birth to my first-born child," She continued to tell her story.

We learned a lot from listening to our elders. The Charity Hospital was located on Texas Street before it was rebuilt on Kings Highway. The name was changed to Confederate Memorial Medical Center. It was the health care facility for the poor or for indigent care. Most of us were not financially able to obtain health care coverage.

As we conversed we had uninvited guests, intruders, or pests. Mosquitoes barged in and attacked us. The females are known to suck the blood of man. I told my young siblings our grandfather had a remedy. He kept the grass cut in our yard and he used a garden hoe to do it. After it dried, Papa raked the grass into several piles to be used as a smoke deterrent for mosquitoes. He had no lawn mower. *John Burr's* invention was not available to us at that time. Grandfather built a fire and covered it with dried grass to make it smolder. He smoked the mosquitoes away. All the children thought that was amazing.

"How did he know to do that?," Dinah asked.

"Our elders had a way of doing whatever they needed to do," I replied.

"We did not have "*off spray*" or any other repellent to ward off the mosquitoes. It was unheard of," I explained.

"Our forefathers had a remedy for everything. They believed in prayer and they trusted God to provide whatever was needed," I continued my explanation.

God made a way then, and He is still making a way. We learned a lot while living in the country. Other creatures: frogs and toads were plentiful. Frogs have bulging eyes and they make croaking sounds. The toad is usually brown in color and his skin is dry and rough. We were told, "Don't let them pee on your hands because you'll get warts on them." Frogs are usually covered with warts. Some frogs live in water and on land. They are amphibians but some stay away from water. Many toads live in the woods. As we gathered wood for the fireplace and the wood burning stove, we encountered brown frogs. They were always seen during the spring and summer because they hibernate in the winter.

The owl is a creature of the night; it is called the "*night watchman*." It has binocular vision and can be heard from quite a distance. We heard its distinctive sounds as we sat on the porch at night. It makes several loud hoots: whoo, whoo whoo. Therefore, we called it a "*whoo owl*." Perhaps owls were in the woods because we detected the sound from the leman woods, which were behind our house. Owls are known to feed on rats. It is remarkable to think about how animals survive. Every animal depends upon another animal for food. That means every animal watches out for its own life because it is subject to be eaten by another.

The thick "*leman woods*" were beside highway 1.

"Don't walk down that stretch of the highway at night because it's dangerous," Cousin Jack said as if he were afraid.

Within minutes, he revealed something else.

"A lot of men were hanged in the leman woods," He said with the sound of anger in his voice.

Many evil workers do their dirt in the dark but it is a fact that God has an all-seeing eye. He neither slumbers nor sleeps. What ever is done in the dark will come to the light.

Death of a Neighbor

Late one night we were all in bed and something happened. Our neighbor's husband died. Mrs. Sarah was married to Mr. Eugene West. They lived just down the road within walking distance from us. They were related to my godmother. However, in the country everybody walked from one house to another. Not many plantation residents owned cars. Mrs. Sarah's house was the closest one to ours. It was about two city blocks away.

"Mr. Eugene died while sitting on the front steps of his house. He had one hand on the banister," Mom said, while shaking her head.
She was saddened by the news.
"What happened to him?," We asked simultaneously.
They really don't know, Said Mom."

We were never told if he died of natural causes, but we were afraid just because he died. We were still afraid after the funeral. Every time I walked past Mrs. Sarah's house, I paused and remembered Mr. Eugene. I did that many times. I pictured him sitting on the steps just as Mom had said, and I thought Mrs. Sarah was going to die soon.

"*Children, I ain't gonna live long*," She said.
"How does she know that?," I began to wonder.
"Does she know something that we don't know," I continue to think.

We were afraid of the dead, so we slept with our heads under the cover. We thought Mrs. Sarah might die any day and we were expecting to hear what we called, "*bad news.*" Every day for quite some time, we inquired about the elderly woman. Nevertheless, she lived many years after her husband's death. She was perhaps a hundred years old or older.

As I recalled there was a graveyard not far from the house where Mrs. Sarah lived. It was not the one in, which Mr. Eugene was buried. We were told a Caucasian family was buried there. Some of the headstones were very large and unusual. Grandfather kept the cemetery clear of overgrown brush, grass, and other debris. Sometimes he brought an opossum home.

"Opossums are found in cemeteries because they eat the bodies of the dead," Cousin Mary said, as if she knew.

"How could that be?," I asked.

"Those bodies were placed there many years ago. Surely there are only skeletons in the graves," I replied.

But that's what they do, said Cousin Mary."

"How do you?," I asked.

"I just know," she said.

I concluded opossums might eat the bodies of the dead, but they do not rely upon the dead for survival. Anyway, we ate the opossum. We also ate black birds. Grandpa set traps for them during the winter when lots of snow was on the ground. He used two boards, one of which he attached to a heavy string. Somehow, he pulled the string through a window and when the birds entered the trap to feed, he pulled the string, which released the top board on the birds. He caught them, cleaned and cooked them, and we ate them! That was good meat. It just was not enough. Some of our neighbors ate armadillos. Cousin Eloise cooked an armadillo and brought a portion to us.

"Taste this, it's just like chicken," Said Eloise.

"It looks like chicken," I responded.

"It tastes good," Said Eloise.

I took a bite of it and I said, "Hum, I don't know if it tastes ju-st like chicken."

Well, it had the appearance of fried chicken, but I really do not know what it tastes like. Armadillos are strange looking creatures with hard shells. They can dig a hole, go under ground, and hide in a matter of minutes. Dallas was Papa's black dog. He tried desperately to reach an armadillo, which was underneath our house in a hole. Dallas barked, barked and barked, but the armadillo would not budge.

One summer day, Dallas left home and stayed away a long time. We thought he was dead, but he returned. We greeted him as if he were a family member. We lived in the country and there was plenty of room to roam. I do not know how long Dallas lived but he was around a very long time.

Dad Returned

Dad came by to see what was going on as if it were his business. He did not seem to be concerned but just curious. He asked many questions. Sometimes he came by and his "*bold*" mistress was with him. She remained in the car. That was a good idea. Dad came by, but he never brought anything to show his concern for our well-being. He never gave us any money, nor did he ask if we were in need of anything. Perhaps he wanted to patrol the area every now and then. He also wanted to know if another man was visiting Mom. There were times when Dad showed up at our house without his mistress. He wanted to control Mother's life from a distance. Just maybe he thought he was still our "*task-master*" too.

Happiness with Grandpa

Grandfather owned an old car. Maybe it was a Hudson. He did not drive but Uncle Ellis could drive. Uncle carried us to Sunday school and church sometimes and he showed us a hard time too. Many Sundays we walked to church because Uncle was not always available, and Grandfather did not always have a car. When Uncle carried us to church, he drove carelessly, thus stirring our emotions. He knew we were afraid and he seemed to get a thrill from hearing us scream. We asked him to slow down but to no avail. Uncle had not accepted Jesus Christ as his Lord and Savior. Therefore, he did not go to church with us. Mother was an usher at Mount Olive Baptist Church, and Grandpa was a deacon. The ushers wore white uniforms in the spring and summer. They wore black uniforms with white detachable collars in the fall and winter. Mother fashioned many uniforms for herself and others. She did a very good job without the use of a pattern. She cut fabric *freehand*. I was a junior usher! During the annual association, all the churches in the area sent two delegates to represent their congregation.

Association @ a Local Church

Being at home with my grandparents was great. Grandfather helped all of us with our arithmetic. He loved to call out columns of numbers and tell several of us to add them up.

"What's the total?," He asked. They must tally, girls," He said.
"What is tally, Grandpa," I asked.
"That means everybody gotta have the same answer," He explained.
"What you got?," he asked."
We stated our answer one at a time. When all of us answered the same, Grandpa said,
"You got it, you got it girls."
"That's good," He continued.

We laughed and clapped our hands. Grandpa helped us to increase our knowledge of addition, subtraction, multiplication and division. We did not know at that time, but we realized later that Grandfather was encouraging us to be competitive. It was fun to be with him. He told us stories about his early life and he loved to play games. He hid cakes in odd places and told us to find them. We looked around and about the house. When we walked close to the hidden cake, Papa would say, *"You're hot."* When we walked away from the hidden treasure, he would say, *"You're cold."* We shared the cake after it was found.

At night, we sang songs to him. I was one of the smallest but I was always ready to be the song leader. The songs were always spiritual.

"That's good! That's good!," Said Papa, while rubbing his head.
I laughed and responded with a clap for myself.

Grandpa always encouraged us to work hard and do well. We were happy with him and he kept us laughing. We called Grandfather *"Papa."* All the grandchildren loved to play with him. He owned a large unusual trunk, which had a lock built into it. That meant he had a key to it. The trunk also had a tray with sections in it. He stored important papers and valuables there. The family Bible was one of his treasures. It contained information about each family member: birthdays and deaths. Mom usually recorded that information.

"I got land in Mansfield, Louisiana and some in Houston, Texas," Said Papa.
One day we were discussing the land.

"Papa told me I can have the land in Mansfield," Said Miriam.
That's mine, She continued.
"Oh yeah, he said that land is for Miriam," Esther added.

Perhaps his deeds were stored in the trunk too. I am not sure about how he acquired the properties, but I recall something about a woman, Anne Latson. Mr. L. X. Williams lived in Shreveport, La. He visited Papa occasionally. They talked about the land, which Papa owned, and Papa paid his taxes every year.

Papa had several brothers, Walter, Noble, Matt, Beaulow and one sister, Louisa. Uncle Matt had a set of twins: Mary and Martha. One of Papa's nephews was Judge Clarkson. His wife was Lucille Anderson-Clarkson. She was a dear friend to our mom and she came to visit often. We called her Cousin Cille, and we addressed her husband as Cousin Honey. She loved greens and Mom cooked them seasoned with salt meat, and she baked cornbread for her. We crumbled our bread up in the greens and ate with our fingers. We had silverware, but we chose to eat *greens* with our fingers. Mom baked whole sweet potatoes and they were sweet. They were so sweet, we notices the sticky syrup after it ran out of the potatoes! Papa raised corn and we cooked it on the cob in a big black teakettle. It was good! We also had our own popcorn.

Uncle Ellis brought Papa to Shreveport to see a doctor concerning cataracts on his eyes. He visited his brother-in-law. Uncle Buck had a shop on Milam Street where he shinned shoes. It was not far from El Grottos Club. Mother went to Mattie Ruth's Beauty Shop on Milam Street. The shop was situated on a hill. Aunt Mattie and Uncle Charlie lived on Picket Street in a little shotgun house. When Mom came to town, she took advantage of the opportunities to visit. Sometimes she spent the night with Aunt Mattie when she had an appointment at Confederate Memorial.

An interesting thing about Grandpa was his "*hair.*" It was so straight there was not a kink in it. One could comb his hair with any little hair comb and it would just glide through it. We loved to comb his hair. Mr. Arthur Morris was his barber. His brother, Matt resembled him a lot and he had a nice grade of hair too. Uncle Matt's wife was Parthine Dale-Clarkson. Uncle Noble was married to Pearl. Thanks to Mr. Walter Sammons for his invention of the *hair comb*. By the way, he was a black man.

My mother once told me that her family was descendants of Indians. Interesting enough, some of our relatives on Mom's side of the family had long beautiful hair. Some had beautiful skin and high cheekbones. Perhaps they were distant relatives of Indians. They were known to have long hair. Every family should research their roots. It is interesting to know about our descendants and discover what is in our genes (the basic unit of heredity).

As a little girl, I dreamed often. I sat down with Papa and told him all about them.
"You watch that," he said while rubbing his head.

It is common for children to dream. I recall Joseph was the youngest son of Jacob and he was a dreamer. Therefore, that was nothing new. I was so young and I did not know just how to analyze a dream. I wondered what the meaning was. I was just a child and had not acquired wisdom but was serious-minded.

"Are they dreams or visions?" I asked very seriously.

"Just watch them," said Papa.

I heard my mom say when she dreamed about fish somebody was going to have a baby. Usually, somebody in the family or an acquaintance was pregnant, but we did not hear the word *pregnant* during that time. I am aware that not all dreams have a significant meaning but many dreams are warnings of things to come. We might dream or experience nightmares after overeating. The same might happen to patients after ingesting certain drugs or multiple medications.

Another Lesson Learned

Our grandfather used garret snuff. He usually poured some into his bottom lip from his big brown bottle. He kept a little round tin can of snuff in his pocket. Sometimes he kept his snuff on a ceil, a small shelf, which was just beneath the porch. Rachel could also dip the strong snuff. I recall a different kind, which was called sweet snuff, but both had a strong odor. Rachel was little, mischievous, and she loved to boss. She had the nerve to tell me that she could give me a dip of snuff. Evidently, I did not think it was a bad idea because I decided to try it, or maybe it was the association. Miriam held my lip out while Rachel poured the snuff into it. I was taller than Rachel was but I stood there like a little dummy and instead of closing my eyes, I was trying to see how much she poured into my lip. Unfortunately, *snuff* got into my eyes.

"Oh, oh, oh!" I cried as I jumped up and down.

My eyes were burning so badly all I could do was holler. Rachel ran and got a wash-pan of water and an old dress. Miriam tried to wash my face in hopes of removing the snuff from my eyes. I learned a good lesson: Do not allow anyone to encourage you to do what you think is wrong. I did not dare try to dip snuff again.

At Gun Point

Mother's mom, Grandma Dolly was a stout woman with big hips. She had a twin brother, Scarborough. He was a little man. Of course, they were fraternal twins. Grandma wore an apron every day and she kept a rag tied around her head with the bow at the back. Her hair was always braided Indian style, which meant two long braids could be seen hanging down. Grandma looked every bit like an Indian and she spoke with authority.

She stood in front of the window in her room with her arms folded as she looked outside. The window was one of those wooden cutouts that could be pushed open like a door. While standing there she mumbled to herself. I often wondered what she was saying, and to whom was she speaking. I did not dare question her!

One day her son, Uncle Ellis came by and he was as drunk as a skunk. The elite would say he was inebriated. He was crying like a baby and no one could understand a word he said. He laid out on the floor.

"Get him up, and take him home," Said Grandma.

We looked from one to the other. We were wondering, "Has she lost her mind?"

We were little and we could not handle Uncle, but when Grandma spoke, she meant what she said. My cousins and I struggled with Uncle and the more we pulled to get him up, the more he cried. We could not move him an inch. It was like tug of war! Grandma went and got the shotgun!

"Get him up!," She said with a commanding voice.

We were scared but somehow we were able to get him upon his feet and we started down the road toward his house. Maybe Uncle was afraid Grandma was going to start shooting the gun. Something triggered his thinking and we were glad. Finally, we made it to his house and we told Aunt Sister what Grandma said to us. After all the drama, we were relieved. However, it was a common thing for Uncle to get sloppy drunk. One day he fell into the fireplace. Apparently, his thinking had been impaired because of the amount of alcohol, which he had consumed. Uncle could not remove himself from the fire. One of his hands burned badly, but two of his grandchildren were there. They went into that room not knowing what was happening. They called their grandma who came to his rescue. I am sure he was *glad she did.* Things could have been much worse. Uncle was treated for burns and skin was also drafted to his hand.

Mr. Mot Bailey was a big, fat man who lived in the house, which was vacated by Mrs. Sarah West after her husband died. He probably weighed about 400 pounds. He sat on the porch with a walking cane in his hand, and he sold *moonshine liquor.* Uncle may have bought alcohol from him. Mr. Mot had a wife, Mrs. Coot. She was a dark complexioned woman who stuttered when she spoke.

"Mr. Boss asked me, Dooooo you know how to iron?,"said Mrs. Coot.

"I told him I can suit myyyself," She continued.

"I wasn't gonna iron for him,"She said.

"He went on 'bout his bbbbbusiness too," She remarked.

One day Rachel and I went to Aunt Sister's house to borrow a cup of Mrs. Tucker's shortening. I was afraid to go alone because Auntie had a cock, which was sure to fight. He hid underneath the little wooden steps to the front of the house. The cock waited until we were about to enter the house then jumped out and attacked us. Since we were aware of the crazy cock, we learned to walk almost to the house and call out to Auntie. She came outside and protected us. The cock would attack anyone as if it were a German shepherd or a bulldog. Maybe there was some type of mix-up with the cock. That was a strange rooster! We should have placed him in contests around the country. Maybe we could have entered him at the "*state fair.*" Perhaps he would have earned us some money.

A House to Call Home

In 1952, we moved into our own little shotgun house on the plantation. Uncle and his wife had lived there previously, but they saw an opportunity to move into a larger house and they took advantage of it. The house, which we moved into belonged to the plantation owner but we called it our own. It was one of those little houses, which one could stand on the porch and look all the way through from the first room to the last one. The house had only three rooms and the roof was tin. When it rained we could hear the water hitting the tin top like popcorn popping, but it was music to our ears. We grabbed a quilt and spread it on the floor. It was naptime and we curled up and slept as hard as the rain hit the tin top. There were times when the roof leaked. Mom placed a bucket underneath the trickle of water. Sometimes it was necessary to move furniture around to prevent it from getting wet. Even in our frustration, we did not lose hope. One might recall II Corinthians 4:8 *We are troubled on every side, yet not distressed; we are perplexed, but not in despair.*

We know that God sends the rain to water the grain, to cool the earth, and to supply us with water for many purposes. If we read Leviticus 26:4, we will be reminded: ...*Then I will give you rain in due season and the land shall yield her increase, and the trees of the field shall yield their fruit.* The scripture is in reference to being obedient to God. We can relax knowing that when the land yields her increase the crops will bring forth an abundant supply: corn, peas, tomatoes, okra and all the veggies, which farmers plant and hope to harvest. When the trees of the field yielded their fruit, there were plenty of peaches, pears, apples and oranges.

"O' taste and see that the Lord is good," Grandma remarked.
"Amen," I concurred.

After the rain, the sun will shine. In addition, after the rain sometimes God allows a rainbow, an arc in the sky to appear. It forms in that part of the sky opposite the sun. After a heavy rain, the rainbow may appear all the way across the sky. Other times it may appear partially across the sky. What a colorful site it is! I wondered why the rainbow displays pastel colors only. Then I thought, several colors appear in each rainbow and the colors blend.

And it shall come to pass, when I bring a cloud over the earth, that the bow shall be seen in the cloud.

Genesis 9: 14 (KJV)

We were grateful to our grandparents, who took us in when we first arrived from Arkansas. Everyone was happy and we had peace-of-mind. Mother purchased her own furniture and we had more food and clothes than ever before. We had been through a *storm of depression* but thank God, we made it. We lived to testify and all of us had a testimony! Mother continued to fashion our wardrobes. She had one of those old-fashioned sewing machines, which had a metal foot piece. Mom worked it like a champion.

It is no wonder I began to sew my own garments after I grew up. I can truly say, *"I am blessed with such a talent."* Praise God from whom all blessings flow! I am now able to purchase a few garments from the *top-of-the-line*. I was thankful for the few things and God blessed me with an abundant supply. Shoes are no longer *hand-me-downs*. Thank God! As a child, I had only one pair of shoes for Sunday's wear and one pair for school. Sometimes I had only one pair. Now I know Mom did the best that she could.

She also had the opportunity to order clothes from Walter Fields and National Belles-Hess Catalogues too. We were elated even though one could stand on the porch and look through the entire little house. That is why it was called a shotgun house. Nevertheless, we were excited! The first room accommodated the old black wood burning heater with its elbow pipe, which extended through the ceiling of the house.

There were no clothes closets as we have today. Mother constructed a place to hang our clothes by nailing a long piece of lumber across one corner of each room. That became our garment rack so-to-speak. It held the clothes and we draped it with a piece of linen, a bed sheet. It took the place of the modern day garment rack. Sometimes long nails were driven into the wall to support single items of clothing such as coats.

Mother owned a chifforobe and a cedar chest. She even purchased a cherry wood four-post bed! It was all beautiful furniture, which was purchased from a store in Coushatta, Louisiana, the nearest town. We still owned the "*iron*" *beds*" too. They were beautifully designed with floral patterns, or tree branches on the head of each piece. Some of them even had an antique finish. They would be very valuable today.

The Kitchen

Our kitchen contained an old four-legged black wood-burning stove. No, it did not have burners like today's ranges. It had four stove eyes, which could be removed. It also contained an oven for baking. Since we had a wood -burning stove there was no monthly gas bill to be paid. We baked bread and cakes. They were the best ones and all from scratch. We did not have cornbread mix or jiffy. Instant foods were not available to us either. The kitchen did not contain nice cabinets like those of today, which are custom built by "M. X. Walker," "J. Bo Builders" or "The Farris Company." Thank God for the little old carpenter, who was exceptionally tall and slender. His name was Sonny Sharp. He came by and constructed a small cabinet without doors attached. It resembled a bookcase attached to the wall. Mother fashioned a curtain to cover it. Oh! We were proud of it and it served the purpose. We thought we were living in style and had earned our way from bondage. It was called "*freedom now*," not "*after-a-while.*" The "*shot-gun house*" was not spacious enough to provide a "*dining room.*" Therefore, we had no "cherry *wood dinette set*," and "*china cabinet*" but we had a table and a few wooden chairs. Many times, we sat on the floor Indian style.

We owned a wooden icebox, which had two doors. The *"ice man"* came by in a truck with a long bed on it. He used a strange looking gadget like a pair of giant pliers to handle the ice. It was purchased by the pound and we always bought 25 or 50lbs. The iceman kindly brought the ice into the house and placed it into the icebox. Mom owned an ice pick. She used it to crack the ice into pieces. Sometimes she chipped off a chunk of ice and placed it into a water pitcher. She made cool aid and we had lemonade when lemons were available. We could always put sugar into the pitcher and make sweet water for a beverage. Perhaps that was called improvising.

Lamp Lights

At that time, there were no electric lights or chandeliers hanging from the ceiling of our house. However, oil lamps with globes were obtainable. The lamp was placed on a shelf or a table. We had the old lantern lights also. They were utilized like flash lights are used today but flashlights were available too. Papa kept at least one big one.

The Floors

They were wood and we scrubbed them clean with *"lye"* water. We used an old broom, which we called a *"nub broom."* We did not always have a mop. Thank God for Mr. Thomas W. Stewart who invented the *mop* and for Mr. Lloyd P. Ray who invented the *dustpan*. Both are beneficial when cleaning floors. Rugs were comparatively a luxury in those days and we could not afford to own one, but we were making progress.

The Walls

We papered the walls with old newspapers to cover the cracks. My siblings will never guess what we used to hang the paper, *"flour batter."* We hanged the beautiful wall covering, which usually consisted of a floral pattern. Wall coverings of today are relatively the same as yesteryears. History does repeat itself.

Floral Pattern Wall Covering

Windows

The windows were square cutouts in the wall and they were pushed open easily. To close them one reached outside and pull it back into its place. While the windows were open, flies, wasps, or any flying creatures had access to the house. When the windows were closed, they were hardly ever noticed. Therefore, there was no need for curtains or drapes. The above photo is one, which was taken years later. A standard window was in the background. Time passed and the carpenter who was ideal for the job came by and installed standard windows like those of today. Mr. Sonny Sharp, the carpenter even finished his job with screen covers. That made it possible to keep the mosquitoes out. Other pests or flies were barred from the house also. We were able to eliminate the mosquito bar, which was placed over the bed at night. We slept with the windows open for fresh air before the standard windows were installed. We were in the country and we felt safe. I would not advise anyone to try that today! The wolves might get them!

Installation of Electricity

Mom was able to purchase a box electric fan to place in the window. We were not blessed with an air conditioner, but thank God for Mr. Frederick Jones, the man who invented the *air conditioner*. Unfortunately, we were still living on Fair Street and had not advanced to Good Avenue. We were happy to see some progress because we had moved from Poor Alley. God blessed Mom to purchase a nice white electric refrigerator and we were grateful for the invention of Mr. John Standard.

Mother purchased a little round electric hot plate. She used it to heat her pressing comb and curling irons. She dressed hair from her home beauty shop and she had many customers. One day she was pressing my hair and Dad appeared. I do not know what prompted an argument, but I remember he hit Mom. She had a good defense weapon in her hand but she did not use it. He may have caught her by surprise. She just cried. She could have left a brand on him but no, she did not try to fight him. The landlord received word from Mom and the police was summoned. Dad was told not to be caught there anymore. A restraining order was issued to him. Thank God! He was not to come anywhere near us because he was a violent man! Well, we were relieved temporarily. It was indisputable that he left Arkansas in order to monitor our whereabouts as well as our actions. I often wondered why he aggravated us. He had his mistress and Mom did not interfere with them. Dad was very unfair! He practiced double standards.

The Yard–Landscape

We had beautiful flowerbeds; sunflowers were the tallest one could imagine. They were big yellow flowers, which had brown centers. They were reminders of smiling faces with bright eyes glowing like "*sunshine.*"

Zinnias were colorful and the thought was, we are people of diverse races whether red, yellow, brown, pink or white, we can live together. We can do whatever we choose and have harmony continuously. That is, if we love one another. Then there was also the flower: "*ice on the mountain,*" which grew tall and slender. It grew taller than most flowers that are grown in flowerbeds. At the very top, it was white, characteristic of snow on a mountain's peak. Consider what it might demonstrate: "Stand, no matter what your stature is. Stand and hold high your hopes of obtaining your goals." Faith is the substance of things hoped for; the evidence of things not seen. To break it down: Faith is trusting God for everything. Of course!

The morning glory" greeted us: "Good Morning, this is the day which the Lord has made, let us be glad and rejoice in it." The *"four o' clock flower"* did not dare forget its purpose. At four o' clock p.m., the day had begun to end. Most of the work had been done. Therefore, the flower slowly brought its petals together for it was time to close up, fold up until the next day. It was an opportunity to take a break from the action, time to unwind. Rest was essential. The daily tasks were not always easy however; it was a fact that we had to work.

A Variety of Work

We had our own little garden and it contained plenty of vegetables. Grandpa used a plow, which was drawn by a mule to prepare the soil for growing veggies. We had butter beans, corn, plenty of purple hull peas and crowder peas. Mom planted squash too. There was the crooked neck yellow squash and the white squash, which resembled a flying saucer. We grew very large sweet potatoes and I was amazed. It was even more amazing to cut the potato vines at a notch, tie a knot in them, and replant them. I loved to harvest the potatoes. We dug them up from the ground with a garden hoe in September or October of the year. We also had a grub hoe for digging.

We had plenty of okra and it grew voluntarily in the cotton field every year. One day I was picking okra, gathering tomatoes, and praying to God like an adult. Aunt Sister was in the field also, but I did not see her. She heard me praying.

"Hey, I was wondering who that was just- ah- praying," She said while smiling as if she were pleased.
"It's me and I was thinking about so many things," I said surprisingly. Jehovah God, our supplier kept food on our table. Mom prayed and her prayers were answered. I prayed too because I was thankful.

Preparing food for the winter was indeed a task but fun. We preserved fruits and canned vegetables. Successful home canning depended upon the selection of fresh food in perfect condition. Overripe or damaged fruits and vegetables were not canned or preserved. Food was sorted and graded according to size and stage of ripeness. Absolute cleanliness was essential. Fruits and vegetables were washed several times to remove all soil and grit. All blemishes, tough peels, and hulls were removed completely. Tomatoes were dipped into boiling water until the skin loosens, then we put them into cold water to make them easier to handle. We peeled them.

Mother "dear" & Cousin Ella D.
Studying God's Word, Sunday School Lesson

There are two methods of preparing food for canning, raw packing and hot packing. The raw pack was simpler and the results were good or better than the hot or precooked pack. More precooked than raw food could be packed into a jar. That was important especially since storage space was limited. Mom stored canned food out of sight underneath the bed. For successful canning, it was important to have equipment in perfect condition. All containers, lids except those with sealing compounds and rubber rings were washed in hot soapy water and rinsed until thoroughly clean. Containers were filled quickly to keep the precooked food hot. After the jars were filled, the rubber rings and the sealing edges were carefully wiped clean because food on the sealing surface could prevent an airtight seal. In some cases, space was left between the packed food and the top of the container. To ensure safe canning the proper method of processing was used for each type of food. Mother taught us well and we did a good job. We gathered food in the spring and summer and we prepared it for the fall and winter. We followed the example of a tiny creature, the ant that stores food in the summer for the winter.

> *Go to the ant, thou sluggard; and consider her ways, and be wise. Which having no guide, overseer, or ruler, Provideth her meat in the summer, and gathereth her food in the harvest.*

> Proverbs 6:6-8 (KJV)

Fishing

Mother went fishing often. She caught brims and sometimes she brought white perch home. One day she went fishing and the fish were not biting.

"I asked the Lord to let me catch just two for dinner and I will leave," She said.

She came home happy because she had two large white perch. They were enough for a meal. She cleaned them herself and fried them. They were just what she asked for. We went fishing not for pleasure but with intention of bringing home fish for dinner. One morning Ruth and I went to try our luck. We had earthworms, which we dug up from the earth and placed in a can. Some of them were brown and others were red. We used them to bait our fishing hooks. I had a time trying to do that because they wiggled around. Some people used sawyers on their hooks. They were a different type of worms. There was a lake near Cousin Aples Gibson's house, which was not far from Mount Olive Baptist Church. We had our own fishing canes. Each line had a cork stopper, which floats on the water and a piece of lead near the hook to make it sink in the water. When we chose to fish deep, we pulled the cork back to allow the hook to fall deeper into the water. When the cork barbed up and down we knew a fish was nibbling on the bait. On that particular day, I threw my line across a large log that was partially in the water. Then I sat down. Within a few minutes, I noticed movement of my line. I pulled on the cane and surprise, surprise; a big *"cat fish"* was on my line. It was so large it frightened me. I forgot everything for a few seconds and took off running. When I realized I was still holding my fishing cane I dropped it and kept running. My big sister took care of the fish. I was finished almost as quickly as I had started. I do not remember if Ruth caught any other fish that particular day, but I had enough excitement for one day. I did not have the nerves to put the fishing line into the pond again.

Papa was a fisherman also. He walked to Red River, which was just across the levee. He did not use a fishing cane. He had a long line and several hooks were attached about two feet apart. He carefully placed earthworms on each hook before he cast the line into the river. Papa set the line into the ground and returned about two days later to either find fish, or discover the line was still empty. One day he returned home injured. He had removed his line and somehow a hook penetrated through the skin on top of one of his hands. Someone transported him to Dr. Huckabay's office where the hook was removed.

Cousin Eva was my grandfather's niece. She called him Uncle Munchie. I never knew why and she had another idea of catching fish. Usually after a thundershower, Cousin Eva would roundup adults and children to go to the bayou. They went seining. The grown-ups went into the pond and let down a large net. The children got into the water to make it muddy in hopes of running the fish into the net. Cousin Eva knew what she was doing because they caught many fish and divided them with each family. Wow! that was amazing. We did not participate in the seining because Mom was afraid for us to get into the pond. We could not swim but Cousin Eva told us to mud crawl. Mom did not think it was safe.

"You'll can't get into the bayou," She said softly.
That meant we could not go with the crew. Cousin Eva and the crew were not fishermen like Peter and Andrew, disciples of Jesus who were brothers. These two disciples were fishers by trade. Jesus said unto them, *"Follow me and I will make you fishers of men."* We are to become fishers of men also. We learned to do that.

We did virtually everything that one can visualize taking place on a farm. I loved what we did and was fond of it. That was our way of life. It was hard work and I would not want to repeat any of it. The discarded items from the kitchen table were called slop. One day I was trying to pour the slop into the trough when the hog jumped up and knocked the tin fence against me. It cut my left foot. I could not wear my shoes for a number of days. I did not go to the doctor, but Mom was told to put a piece of fat meat on a rag and tie it around my foot. I do not know what else was used for healing, but I thanked God my foot healed. The scar is evidence, it remains today and it is a reminder of *"country living."*

We did a variety of things like gathered and sold pecans when they were in season. Someone would climb the trees and shake the pecans off. Mom said that was called thrashing the trees. We gathered the pecans and filled grass or croker sacks, which were carried to the store to be weighed. The man who thrashed the trees was given a portion of what each person gathered. We were paid a small price for each pound but we were thankful for whatever it was.

Chickens

We raised chickens. They are considered to be birds and they were raised for meat and eggs. Thank God, two chickens were on the Ark, which Noah built. Chicken is one of the most popular meats for dinner, snacks or whenever. It can be prepared so many ways. There were two of every animal aboard the ark. I recall a funny or strange chicken. It was speckled and Mom called it a guinea. Hens always made their own nests and laid their eggs in them. Sometimes when a nest was discovered, it already contained a half dozen eggs or more. When it was noticed that a hen was setting on her eggs in order to keep them warm and eventually hatch little chicks, Mom used a lead pencil and marked each egg. She did that to be able to distinguish those eggs from any fresh ones, which were laid in the nest later. All fresh eggs were removed as soon as possible. We knew when an egg had been laid because the hen cackled. That was an announcement. The roosters pecked and scratch in search of food and after a number of days, the hen had finished her job. She had a group of fluffy yellow chicks and she clucked over them. She was very protective of her little ones. One day we were playing outside and Anna saw the little chicks all in a row.

"Yow!," She said. She was so excited.
"Ah ha ha ha," Anna burst into laughter.

She was tempted to grab one of them. They were as cute as could be. There were about eight or ten of them. She grabbed one of the little chicks and to her surprise; the hen begin pecking her hand.

"Put it down Anna, put it down!," I yelled.

She was still holding the chick, and the hen was constantly attacking her.

"Let it go Anna," I said.

Anna still held on not understanding that as long as she held the baby chick the hen would attack her. Finally, after the hen hurt her, she realized, "I better put this baby down."

The girl did not dare do that again. In fact, she ran the opposite way when the hen and her little ones were parading around on the yard. Everywhere the hen went, the little ones were right behind her.

"Ah-ha-ha-ha!," She chuckled.

She could hardly resist the temptation, but she remembered what happened the last time she grabbed one of the hen's babies. She had scars on one of her hands.

A hen doth gather her brood under her wings.

Luke 13:34 (KJV)

It was eye-catching when the hen was in the yard and her little chicks were right behind her everywhere she went. They knew how to follow the leader. That was a common barnyard site.

It is amazing how the contents of an egg become a chick! I had an opportunity to watch a chick emerge from the shell. That was awesome and the shell was left clean. Mom had brought some eggs inside the house because it was cold. She placed them beside the fireplace. They were warm, the shells cracked, and the little chicks emerged. I could not ignore my thoughts about the awesomeness of God.

At the end of every day the chickens went inside the chicken house and perched themselves on limbs, which had been put in place for that purpose. The chickens flew out of their little house early in the morning. The early morning crowing of roosters has served farmers as alarm clocks for many years. Strangely, we were told when a child had chicken pox he got rid of them by allowing the chickens to fly over his head. I do not know how much truth is to that. However, we tried it!

The Swine Thief

We had an unusual hog, which would steal. The swine went to Cousin Eva's house and grabbed a fishing cane. He brought it to our house. Mom did not tolerate stealing but she could not discipline the swine.

"Do you think the animal is strange?," I asked the girls.
They looked from one to the other and replied, "O' yea, yea he is strange."
"He is an unusual hog," I concluded.
"Huh, huh huh," The girls chuckled simultaneously.

We thought he was very strange, a rare breed.
He was trying to tell us, "You can use the cane to catch fish; you don't have to get into the bayou." He seemed to be smart after all.

My imagination was magnified! I thought maybe we should have inquired about IQ tests for strange animals. The results may have revealed reasons to spare the swine. Nevertheless, it did not happen. The swine was not a pet, so he did not receive royal treatments. He could not escape the slaughterhouse, even though he appeared to be clever. He was destined for the dinner table and his brilliant skill could not save him.

Chapter 9

Life in Louisiana

In early spring, the men who lived on the plantation used heavy equipment, machinery and etcetera to cultivate the land. Tractors provided the chief source of power. Machinery was used to plant the crops after the land was broken up. By the way, the tractor replaced the horses and mules for drawing plows, combines, planters and other machines. The cotton was planted and after a few weeks, there was evidence. It grew crowded and in long straight rows according to the length of the field. Shortly thereafter, it was time to get the tools out from beneath the houses. In the country, all houses were built up off the ground on blocks of some sort. They were not built on concrete slabs as most houses of today are.

During the summer, we chopped cotton in the fields. When the truck with the long bed came by our house, we boarded it like a bunch of slaves. We used the garden hoes and a file was kept close by in order to sharpen them when they became dull from continuous use. There was always a handyman to perform that duty. We adorned ourselves in layers of clothing to protect our skin from the hot sun. Even though we wore long sleeved shirts and big sun hats like Mexicans, it was obvious that we had been working in the field. We had a tan! We chopped cotton to thin it out and remove any grass or weeds that grew with it. One day Rachel was chopping cotton beside me and she was raising her hoe too high. She accidentally hit one of my knees leaving a nick on it. Miriam was chopping cotton along with us too. Chopping cotton was a joint effort. When one worker fell behind the group, the foreman helped that person to catch up by chopping a "*skip in his row.*" Working in the field was a way of life. The weather was hot and we were thirsty often. A young boy walked through the field carrying a pail of water with a dipper in it. We called him the "*water boy.*" He walked from one person to another and everybody drank from the same dipper. We never thought about spreading germs from one person to another. But God protected us.

In August, we picked cotton without the presence of a "*task master*" with a whip at hand. Sometimes each family was assigned to pick cotton in a certain section of the field. We filled our cotton sacks, carried them to the end of the field, and emptied them on a large sheet. The cotton was weighted at the end of the day. Many times each family was assigned a cotton field to work. We had a "*cotton house*" in which we emptied our sacks as often as we chose. At the end of the year we were paid. We thought we were paid. The boss called that a settlement.

One strange thing happened. There was a woman who carried a saddlebag. She dressed very unusual, looked peculiar, and rumors were that she carried roots in her bag. We were not comfortable when she was around. When she looked at us, her eyes seemed to penetrate to the core. We wondered, "Why would anyone carry a saddle bag in a cotton field?" The "*bag lady*" did, although we thought it was weird!

Many times, we filled our sacks and packed the cotton down in order to put more into them. We used our feet to pack the sacks tightly. Many times, I could not lift my sack by myself after it was filled. I called someone to give me a lift. Sometimes I fell to the ground with the sack after I was given a lift. Finally, the sack was placed on my shoulder. I put my hand on my hip to help balance it. I carried it to the scales to be weighed. By the way, a green cotton bulb was wired into one corner of each sack to hang it on the scales before it was given to the user. Our names were written on our sacks also. The wire was looped onto the scales and the strap of the sack was wrapped around the top portion of the scales. Mr. Ward weighted the cotton and kept the record for everybody. Mom always kept her own record to figure how much cotton we had picked. There were always two men in the trailer to empty the sacks. When one trailer was filled, it was carried to the gin and another trailer replaced it. The most I ever picked was 205 pounds in one day. That was a job. We were paid only *$2.00 per hundred.* That was oppression! We were still working as slaves in the 1950s.

Another pharaoh was the commander in chief. At the end of the day, my back hurt.

"You don't have a back, you only got a gristle," Mrs. Holly said.

Regardless of what she said, my back hurt. My fingers hurt too. They had snags around the cuticles from grabbing cotton from the bolls. We picked cotton, cotton and more cotton! Most times, I picked from one row. Many of our elders picked from two rows. Sometimes two adults picked from three rows. Each person was responsible for picking from one row in addition to picking from a row in the middle. We called that "*snatch row.*" When the cotton became scarce, we pulled the whole bole of cotton off. That was after the announcement was made, "*It's time to pull cotton.*" That was hard for me to do, but I tried it.

Farm Chickens with coop in the rear

Food Preparation

Occasionally we caught one of the young pullets after running it down. We put it into a little house called a *coop*, an enclosed cage for fowls.

We fed it corn and gave it water, which contained Epsom salt, hydrated magnesium sulfate. That was used as a cathartic to evacuate the bowels or clean it out. After a few days, one of us checked the young pullet by feeling its thighs to determine if it was getting fat. After a number of weeks in the coop, we took the chicken out, not to let it go free but to prepare it for Sunday's dinner. Ruth was always the one to stir our emotions by wringing the chicken's neck. She took its head off! Then the chicken flopped around until it was dead. It could not see nor determine which way to go. That is why some people make the statement, *"running around like a chicken with no head."* Next step: she dipped the chicken into hot water, picked the feathers off, and singed it by subjecting it into flames in order to remove remaining stubs. Then she was ready to use the big kitchen knife to finish it off. She cut it open and cleaned it out. The big bird was taken through the final step of preparation.

Sunday's meal was delicious: Smothered chicken, seasoned greens with pork strips, candied yams, cornbread and lemonade. The crock bowl was filled with teacakes. Speaking of greens, Esther had a digestive problem when she was very young. She could not ingest greens without getting sick. She had so *many* problems. Thank God, she can tolerate them today!

I do not recall such a meal while struggling to live with Dad, but we thank God, who is able to do exceeding abundantly above all that we ask or think. Circumstances changed tremendously after we moved back to Louisiana. We did better without a man in the house. He was a hindrance to us. To God be the glory for things He has done!

A Sight for Sore Eyes

Mom raised hogs to have our own meat to put on the table. We always slaughtered a hog in the winter. We asked for help from several men who lived in the community. It was a group project. A fire was started around the big black pot of water. It was used to remove the hair from the hog after it was killed. A slaughtered hog was a sight to see because it was hung up with its belly cut open. The hog's small intestines were cleaned and set aside. They are called chitterlings. I heard Mom talk about *"melt."* I have no idea what that is, but it has something to do with a hog. The hog's head was used to make what we called *"hog head cheese."*

Our grandparents said, "Don't let anybody who is pregnant come near the meat, it will spoil for sure." That did not make any sense to the children, but when grown-ups spoke, they expected cooperation. Sugar cure was used to preserve the pork and it was placed in a smoke house. One would think the meat would have been kept in a freezer, but that was not the case. Many things were done differently years ago. It is amazing how we survived. But God...

Every family within walking distance was given a portion of fresh pork. When the neighbors slaughtered a hog, they returned the favor. We consumed a lot of pork and I did not hear anything about high blood pressure. In fact, we seldom heard about anyone being sick.

Milk on the Farm

While we were living on the Marston Plantation, there were many cattle. The Brahman had a hump on his back and the Herefords were red with white faces. There were the Black Angus and the big bulls. They were in the area where we lived. It was amazing that they were not always in a pasture. It was not unusual to walk down the road to the next house, look back, and see a cow following you. We were told if we wear red, the cows would chase us. I never understood the concept, but it seemed to be true. I tried it and I never ran so hard to reach my destination.

Some of the families had a jersey cow to milk. Surely, the cows did not belong to them, but the overseer allowed them to keep one for a period. The jerseys had large baggy organs, which we called cow bags with long nipples called teats. The cows were milked every morning at dawn. Sometimes after the bucket was filled, the cow kicked it over. I did not understand that. After the cow was milked, someone had the job of churning. The milk was poured into a special container called a churn. The butter dasher is a gadget which resembled a broomstick with a saucer-shaped part about one third of the way near the handle. It was used in the process. One day I was at Mrs. Ward's house when she brought out the milk container, or churn and the butter dasher. She prepared to churn the milk. As she worked the butter dasher up and down in a constant motion, butter collected on the saucer part of the dasher. After a while, she removed the butter and placed it into a bowl. I saw her pour water into it and whip the butter with a fork.

"Why did you put water on the butter?," I asked.
"I am washing the milk out of it," She answered.

I watched her closely because I had never seen anyone churn milk and remove the butter. After she whipped it with a fork, she drained the water off. There she had butter! We did not have a cow but we had milk. Thanks to Mrs. Ward who was our supplier. One day my mom sent me to get a bucket of milk. I had to walk across the cotton field to Mrs. Ward's house. I was wearing my shorts, which I had rolled up a notch higher. I strolled up to the house and her youngest son was outside. He looked at me and smiled as he spoke. I am sure I was blushing. I spoke to him as I went inside. Patty filled my bucket with milk. I thanked her and left the house. As I walked away to go back across the field, I was carrying the bucket carelessly. I thought the young boy was watching me, but I did not dare look back. I dropped the bucket and spilled all the milk. I was afraid but I could not go back and ask for more, so I proceeded to go home. Patty was watching me and she called me to come back for a refill. She told her sister Cookie to walk across the field and carry the milk for me. I was embarrassed and angry with myself because what I did was unnecessary. I did not tell my mom what happened. Each one of us put cornbread in a bowl and poured milk over it. It was good!

Laundry day

We did not have the pleasure of going to a Laundromat. In fact, we did not hear the word "*Laundromat.*" God sent the rain and our cistern always had water in it, or we collected water from a pump. Therefore, we did not have a monthly water bill. How good God is.

Our clothes were washed in a number two or three size round tin tub. One tub was used for washing clothes with "*Octagon*" laundry bar soap. I did not know what laundry detergent was. We scrubbed each item on a laundry board and the second tub was nearby for rinsing the clothes. Bluing is a liquid, which was placed into the tub. After rinsing the clothes, we were ready to hang them on the clothesline with wooden clothespins. We did not own a clothes dryer, which was invented by George T. Sammon. We did not even know it existed. When the line was filled, we used a long pole to prop it up because it began to swag under the weight of the wet clothes. They were left to dry. The bright sunshine and the cool breeze left them country fresh. At the end of the day about four o'clock in the evening, we removed them from the line. The next task was to fold them and put them in their respective places. The job was well done! Sheets and pillowcases were ironed! Yes, they were ironed.

We brought out the large black iron pot, which had four little legs on it. We built a fire around it after it was filled with water. A portion of "*eagle lye*" was poured into it. The white clothes were placed into the pot. As the hot water bubbled, we used a broomstick to poke the clothes down into the pot. The routine was repeated several times. After the process, the white clothes were very clean and white. They were very pretty while hanging on the clothesline. As the wind blew, they seemed to wave and make a popping sound!

The same tin tub, which had been utilized to wash clothes in was used to bathe in. We did not always have deodorant. We used *baking soda* under our arms. Someone knew that it would absorb odors. We brushed our teeth with a mixture of *baking soda and salt* after the toothpaste ran out. That was after we had used a kitchen knife to pull out the last dab.

We also kept a little tub called a foot tub in our possession. We washed our feet in it after walking around barefooted in the summer sand. We did not walk around without wearing shoes just because we enjoyed the feel of sand on our feet. Mom could not always afford to purchase sandals for us.

We had homemade starch, which was made from flour of any brand. Occasionally we had "*faultless*" powder starch but not spray. When we did not have starch, we mixed two cups of flour with approximately one quart of cold water. After mixing it well we poured it into a large dishpan. The next step was to pour boiling hot water into the pan and stir constantly. A lot of water used produced "*thin*" starch, but less water produced "*thick*" starch. We allowed it to stand until it cooled. At that time, it was ready to be used on clothes such as skirts, blouses, shirts, or any items, which one chose to starch.

We had half-slips called "*can-cans.*" They were starched stiff. Other items, doilies or tablecloths were dipped into the starch. We ranged them out, and hung them on the clothesline to dry. After they were removed, we sprinkled them with cold water and rolled them up tightly to be ironed. Sometimes they were placed into the bottom of the refrigerator before time to iron them. I did not know the reason for that. As I reflect, I realize Mom did not want the clothes to mildew. However, after they were ironed they were simply "*beautiful.*" The irons were the "*heavy*" black ones, which were heated in the fireplace or on top of the old four-legged iron stove. After removing them from the fireplace, we were careful to dust the ashes off before using them. We did not dare smudge our work and it really was work! That is the way we ironed before electricity was installed.

The ironing board was a plain board, which had been padded. It was placed across the backs of two chairs. Years later mother purchased an ironing board, which came with its own pad and cover. We were thankful for the work of Ms. Sarah Boone. She invented the *"ironing board."* We were blessed with an electric iron, which made our job easier. Praise God! Our needs were met.

I can truly say, *"Look where He brought us from."*

Spring Cleaning

We always did a very thorough job. We washed the *"cotton stir mattresses."* They were made from heavy material or old cotton sacks and they were open in the middle in order to have space for stirring the cotton around. The bed was made that way daily. While the mattress was drying outside, the cotton, which was the contents, was spread out on a quilt in the sun. At the end of the day, the mattress was brought inside. The cotton was placed back into it and the bed was made nicely. The quilt was rolled up on each side then the roll was turned under. The bedspread was draped neatly on the bed. If we did not own a bedspread a white sheet was used. No one was permitted to sit on the beds. That was an absolute *"No"!* It was really something to behold and identified as amazing country living.

Playtime

Recreation included playing baseball and jacks. When we did not have jacks, we used small rocks. We played tic-tac-toe, seesaw, and we jumped rope. We had several ropes and each person could jump at his own pace. Sometimes two people threw a rope for the others to jump. They ran in one at a time and jumped. Finally, two people jumped at the same time. First, the rope was thrown slowly and after a few minutes, it was thrown very fast. That is what we called *"hot piece."* The objective was to jump rope as long as one could without missing a step. If one accidentally stepped on the rope that person was called out.

Hide-and-seek was another game. Someone sang, "Last night, night before, twenty-four rivals were at my door. I knocked them down with a forty-four. I ain't gonna count but one more time and that is gonna be when the sun goes down. All hid?" Everybody answered, "Y-a-a! The objective was to avoid being found. Usually everybody's hiding place was discovered. If one was not found that person came out of hiding on his own and was declared the winner!

Occasionally we used nub brooms to ride as if we were on horses. We attached two strings to the worn out broom head. We pretended to gallop around the house like *"cowboys,"* who played on Gun Smoke or Rawhide. Our grandfather always wore a hat and he owned several. We used them when pretending to ride a horse. We certainly had vivid imaginations. We had paper cap guns in holsters and we used them.

The swing was hanging from a tree. It was exciting to swing high and feel the cool breeze as we enjoyed the activity. When we chose to slow our pace, we made dolls using soda pop bottles and baling twine, which was called sea grass. That was the *"hair,"* which was held in place by a cork or a corncob. We actually curled the hair. The soda pop bottle doll was popular. Her hair was always long. She was to us what the Barbie doll is to today's generation. We also utilized the wooden thread spools to make dolls.

The playhouse contained broken glass for crystal dishes. The broken brown *"beer bottle"* was also used. It added color to the collection. We made mud cakes and placed them in the *"hot sun"* to dry. After the sun absorbed the moisture, they were stacked and became our layered cakes. That was all *"clean"* country fun. We were still playing with dolls at the age of 12. We sat under the willow tree, dogwood, or peach tree. We enjoyed peaches right in our own back yard. They were good too!

We played something called Little Sally Walker. Several girls joined hands and formed a wide circle. One girl sat in the center. We sang, "Little Sally Walker sitting in a saucer, rise Sally rise, wipe your weeping eyes, put your hands on your hips and let your backbone slip, shake it to the east, shake it to the west, shake it, shake it, shake it until you do your best."

Then the girl in the center chose someone else to become Little Sally Walker. Every girl had a chance to dance. That was fun! We did not have any musical instruments. We used an empty Mrs. Tucker shortening bucket, which we turned upside-down and beat it with our bare hands. That was our drum. The harmonica was a small hair comb. We placed a piece of paper over the teeth and blew air into it. It made a musical sound. Consequently, we discovered ways to entertain ourselves.

Then there were times when we wanted to do something more exciting. We did not have an opportunity to travel to the state of Colorado. In winter, snow of Colorado attracts skiers to famous resorts: Aspen, Estes Parks and Colorado Springs. We never dreamed of climbing the ladder to the top of the *"big slide"* at six flags over Texas. However, we walked to the levee while carrying a big piece of tin. The levee borders the *"sandy"* Red River. The tin was approximately three foot long. Upon arrival, we placed it on top of the levee and each one took turns sliding down the levee on it. That was fun and we could only imagine the fun of skiing at Aspen.

Mother allowed us to watch television at Cousin Eva's house. She lived about a half city block from us. She and Mr. Shine were the first family in the country to own a television set. They had a large family and the children watched with us. It was good entertainment! We watched *rawhide and American bandstand* in the evening. We were not fortunate to purchase a television at that time. However, Mother finally saw an opportunity and took advantage of it. We were so happy to have our own.

Uncle Shorty and his wife came to visit with us. I loved him dearly. Many times I wished he were my dad because he was very supportive of his family.

"How about letting Peanut stay with us a week?," He asked Mom.
"Alright, she can stay," Mom, said agreeing with Uncle.
"We'll bring her back home next weekend," He said.

I was excited about the short vacation. Uncle lived in Shreveport upon a hill somewhere near downtown. He operated a café somewhere in the city. He and Auntie had many children. He seemed to care a lot for his family. He played with the children and I quickly reflected on my life with Dad. Auntie cooked good meals and we ate well! We walked to the *Ritz Theater* downtown and Auntie bought popcorn and drinks for us. We enjoyed the movie, returned home, and talked for hours before going to bed.

Holiday Celebrations

Easter

Mother always designed a beautiful out-fit for each of us. We boiled eggs, dyed them, and my oldest sister hid them. That was the Easter egg hunt. Dinner included our favorite desserts: lemon pie, pecan pie, pound cakes and we always went to church every Sunday. Easter is a reminder of the resurrection of Jesus Christ from the grave.

Juneteenth, a time of commemoration.

We reflected on the arrival of the news in Galveston, Texas that the slaves were free. That was the Emancipation Proclamation. We remembered our deliverance as a people from slavery and those who helped to liberate us. Harriet Tubman, a former slave in America, guided a number of enslaved persons to freedom through the Underground Railroad.

July 4th, Independence Day

An exciting celebration was held. The owner of the plantation was responsible for the dinner. The men who lived on the farm smoked the "*beef,*" which had been slain for the celebration. They dug a large pit, filled it with logs and overlaid it with a net of wire, which held the beef. The men cooked from that particular pit the night before the "*big day.*" One could smell the meat from quite a distance and the aroma aroused one's appetite and brought about exhilaration. On the day of the celebration, we wore short sets or pinafores and sandals. All families were together. The dinner was delicious. Each one's plate was piled high with food. Mom always had her own container to place some of our food into it. She knew we could not consume all the food at one time and she did not want any to be wasted. We had potato chips, pickles and the lemonade was "*ice cold.*" We had a "*good*" time!

Thanksgiving & Christmas Day

The menu was the usual:

> Baked Chicken or Turkey with Dressing
> Cranberry Sauce
> Turnip Greens seasoned with Pork
> Candied Yams
> Cakes: Coconut, Pineapple, Pound Cake
> Lemon & Pecan Pie
> Drinks

A sad time

December 1952, Mom had a young baby, Lois. Therefore, she was not able to go shopping for us. She sent Ruth and Esther with Grandpa and Uncle Cuff who drove his car. Mr. Man was also with them. They left in route to Coushatta, which was the nearest town. After all, it was Christmas time and all the farmers had received their settlement. However, very little money was left after the bill was paid for whatever groceries Mom was billed for during the year. Mom gave Ruth approximately $150.00. She had the money in a little white plastic wallet with pearls or beads on it. When they arrived at Burks Store Ruth purchased a few items, which Mom had instructed her to buy. She also bought a little red rocking chair for Anna. They were ready to return home when Grandpa chose to stop at the fish market.

"Let me have some money to buy some fish," Papa said.

"I don't have any change," He continued.

Ruth said she looked into her little purse and pulled out $10.00. She gave it to Papa and closed the purse. Grandpa went into the fish market and made his purchase. He spent about $5.00, returned and gave Ruth her change. They left Coushatta and when they arrived back home, removed the item from the car, Ruth discovered she no longer had her wallet. She did not know if she dropped the wallet inside the car or what. It was a mystery. It contained the remainder of Mom's money, which was about $90.00. I cannot explain how Ruth felt nor the loss, which Mom dealt with. It was a storm of *misfortune* to say the least.

Toys, fire works and new clothes were expected. On New Years' Day, we always had "*black-eyed peas.*" That was a tradition and it was said that one would have "*good luck*" after eating them. Of course, everyone desired to have "*money*" in his pocket on that day too! On the eve of New Years' Day, we walked outside during the night and showed our money to the moon. I have no idea what that meant. Maybe it was just another thing of the past.

Summer in Pelican, Louisiana

Sometimes during the summer, Dad's mother came to visit. It was not just, because we were her grandchildren. She wanted some assistance with canning or gathering fruits and vegetables. That was her motive. She lived in Pelican, Louisiana and her home was a large "*white house.*" Grandma seemed to be very prosperous and among her possessions were horses, chickens, cattle, and a big garden that she raised. Well, we went home with her and while there, we gathered figs, berries, peaches, pears, and etc. She got just what she wanted. For us it was fun, work, and a change of scenery. Grandma had approximately twenty-five acres of land.

Grandmother Mary Lou owned a large nice house or what I thought was nice. Unlike where we lived, her house had large columns just as you walk up the steps. A beautiful magnolia tree with large white flowers was in the front yard. I thought it was so beautiful.

"One day I will have my own home and I want a magnolia tree in the yard," I said.

Unfortunately, one day I was riding on a slide with my cousins. Two horses dragged it and after they crossed the *old bridge*, the slide turned over and threw me into the bushes. Before it landed upside-down, it struck one of my legs as I lay on the ground. I could not walk for several days and I did not receive any medical care. After I was hurt, for some unknown reason I expected to be given special attention. I even expected to sleep on a bed for a change. To my surprise, no, no, I continued to sleep on a quilt on the floor. Grandma was unfair. She treated us differently from her other grandchildren. As I recall we could not sit on her nice chairs nor sleep on her beds. We sat on the floor except at dinnertime. We sat at the table and we always ate after the adults had eaten. Grandma prepared some good meals and she always had plenty of groceries. I was just amazed and I truly thought she was a rich woman. Surely, many groceries were common, but I came from a poor family therefore, she appeared to be wealthy. After Grandma accomplished her goal, she carried us home. I do not remember if she gave us a jar of fruit for our labor.

Medications & Treatments

Mother gave all of us a dose of castor oil during the winter to help us stay healthy. She made sure it was warm because it is a thick oily substance. It was horrible and it made me nauseated. Esther had an idea. On one occasion when it was her turn to take a dose, she held a towel around her mouth. She poured the castor oil into the towel instead of into her mouth. I did not tell Mom what she did and I do not know if Esther tried that again. Mother also gave us a lemon to remove the unpleasant taste. It did not really remove the taste, but it helped us to tolerate the medicine. Every time I burped, I smelled the castor oil and it just made me sick. We ingested Scott's Emulsion, Grover's Chill Tonic and something called 3

6s or 666. That was horrible also. Maybe all the medications were good for us, but they certainly did not taste good to us. The cow chip tea was nasty, nasty! I do know whose original idea that was, but they could have kept that one to themselves.

Mom had an answer for almost everything. She cooked beef and after it was allowed to cool, the grease settled on top of the meat. She scooped it off, placed into a jar, and stored it away. When one of us was ill with a cold, Mom placed grease called "*tallow*" from the jar on a piece of fabric called outning or flannel. She held the fabric to the fire to heat it, then placed it to our chest before we went to bed for the night. We believe it served the same purpose as Vick's Vapor Rub does today.

Mumps is a disease, which affects the salivary glands. It causes the face to swell. Sometimes just one jaw swelled and the child had a fever. Mom bought sardines in oil and after the child ate the fish, the oil was used to grease his jaw. A piece of fabric was placed under the chin and tied above the head. I do not remember how long the illness lasted. Occasionally, more than one child had the mumps at the same time.

Mom tried to keep us well. Our first cousin, Miriam was stricken with polio. She could not walk for a while. When she recovered, she walked with a limp. Viruses cause poliomyelitis. It is sometimes called infantile paralysis. We thought Miriam might be paralyzed for life. Nevertheless, God saw her through the illness. A vaccine was developed and schoolchildren took part in the tests. We were given an oral vaccine several times during an epidemic. That happened in the mid fifties.

Rachel told me of an incident, which happened in Coushatta.

"I was sick and Papa carried me to the clinic to be seen by a doctor," She said.

"The sheriff came into the waiting room and stated, this is the man I been looking for," She quoted the sheriff.

"He put handcuffs on Papa and I was so scared," She continued as if she were reliving the experience.

"Doctor Huckabay told the sheriff, you got the wrong man. I know him, he hasn't done nothing wrong," She continued to explain the ordeal.

"If it hadn't been for Dr. Huckabay, the sheriff would have carried Papa to jail, and I don't know what I would have done," she said with excitement.

Thank God, for people who speak up when they know the truth. Rachel has one sister, Miriam and a brother, Samuel. Our maternal grandparents supported them. Their dad, Uncle J. deserted them when Samuel was very young. It was a storm of disappointments. Mom was always willing to ensure that they had whatever was needed. If Rachel did not have a slip to wear, Mom gave her one of mine and no question was asked. We shared what we had.

Death of Grandma Dolly

In April of 1955, our grandmother was very ill. She seemed to have so much cold in her chest. Each time she coughed, we heard cold rattle. I wonder did she have pneumonia. Mother and others in the community sat beside her bed all night. Aunt Parthine, Cousin J. B., and Cousin Equilla came to help Mother cared for Grandma many times because she was bedridden. Mother needed all the help she could get. One day grandmother's life ended. She went to dwell in a building of God, a house not made with hands eternal in the heavens. On that day all the grandchildren were at school. Someone came to get us in a pickup truck. We were very sad to hear the news and we sat in the back of the truck in tears. We felt so helpless and we really were.

Funeral Service was held at Elizabeth Baptist Church, West Dale, Louisiana. Grandfather sat beside Grandma Dolly's casket during the service. That was my first and last time seeing anyone do that. I did not understand the reason, but maybe there was a lack of space. The building was very small. I was wearing a lavender dress, which Mom had fashioned some time earlier. I was ten years old and I sat closely beside Mom on the first pew. A few weeks later, Grandpa purchased a headstone and had it placed on Grandma's grave. It was the last thing he could do for her and it was the right thing to do.

Dolly Salters-Clarkson was married to Willie Clarkson. Her parents were Teady Jackson-Salters and York Salters. Both preceded her in death. She had three children: two daughters: Annie Clarkson-Turner, Susie Clarkson-Taylor and 1 son: Ellis Clarkson. Grandma Dolly had several sisters and brothers. Her sisters were, Jo Moore, Hattie Sowsehog, Rachel Perry and Mattie Oliver. Her brothers were, Henry, Bell Hudson and Scarborough Salters. Grandma and Uncle Scarborough were twins. Her sister, Mattie Oliver and brother Scarborough were the last survivors.

Grandma Dolly's brother-in-law, Charlie Oliver was married to Aunt Mattie Oliver. They traveled to California often and he worked as a cement finisher. Uncle Charlie was very nice to Aunt Mattie. She dressed nicely and owned a fur coat, leather gloves and jewelry. They did well during those days. He passed away in March of 1957, two years after Grandma Dolly's death. He had two daughters who lived in Chicago, Illinois. Another chapter was written in Mother's life.

Uncle Bell Hudson

Uncle Bell was a *good-looking, well-dressed man.* He held a cigar in his hand and posed in his big comfortable chair as if he had things in perspective. Uncle's dad was a white man. During that time, it was common for black women to work as housekeepers, cooks and etc. They had no choice but to do as they were instructed. They were sexually assaulted, rapped, and dared to tell or suffer severe consequences at the hand of their slave master. That is one reason our race is one of diverse skin tones: Light skinned, yellowish, red-tone, light brown, brown, dark-brown and black.

Revival

We attended church every Sunday and we had no choice when Sunday school was mentioned. My maternal grandfather always encouraged us and he often said, *"Pay day is coming after a while."* Years later, I realized what he meant. At age10, I was ready to become a member of the church, the family of God. Church service was real. We were not assessed to pay money for anniversaries or any notorious day. The church did not focus on money. We had tribe leaders, who collected whatever the members could pay. During revival, I really prayed earnestly. I was only ten years old but very sincere. The pastor at New Star Baptist Church was Reverend Jack Kemp. Mrs. Ward was a tall stout woman. She could sing solos and hymns very well. I walked up to her, gave her my little hand, and asked her to pray for me and she did. The pastor explained the Word and Mrs. Ward talked with me privately. Today we say *"witness,"* but anyway she got her point across to me and that was important. For that I would likened her to a wise person. I recall something that Solomon wrote.

The fruit of the righteous is a tree of life; and he that winneth souls is wise.

Proverbs 11:30 (KJV)

I had much confidence in Mrs. Ward and she could open up with a song, which made one shiver. She could pray a prayer, which let you know she was in touch with her Master. He is The Great I Am, Jehovah-Jireh, The Provider, El-Shaddai the Lord God Almighty, and Jehovah M Kadesh the Righteous One. While at the coinciding time, tears filled ones' eyes and trickled down his face. The service was very touching and spirit filled. I am reminded: *"Somebody prayed for me."* That someone was Mrs. Ward. I am grateful to

God for He allowed me to cross her path, and I am very thankful for having known her. I believe God brings certain people into our lives for a reason. Sometimes it is to help us see something new and wonderful. Sometimes it is to encourage us and strengthen our purpose. Moreover, it could be just to remind us that we are never alone. Praise God!

The cotton field was my praying ground during the day. I went to revival one Tuesday night and I prayed, and I prayed, and I began to feel good. Suddenly I could not be still. While walking home that night I was happy and the next morning, which was, Wednesday I had to tell somebody that God is real. I believe Jesus Christ is the Son of God. He has saved my soul from a burning hell. I was ready to be baptized. My older sisters and I went from house to house as I told my story, my testimony. As we neared Mrs. Ward's house she saw us coming from a far and apparently, she knew why. As I walked up the steps, I was crying.

"Bring it to me," She said, and grabbed me and held me close.
"I know you got it," She continued as if she was so happy for me.
I believe she was, and I told her all about it. I poured out my little heart.

The day of baptizing was referred to as the *big day*. It only took place once per year and that was during the summer because the water was warm. I was baptized on the 1st Sunday in August in the year of 1955. Some of the deacons of the church went about twenty or thirty feet into the bayou on the Saturday before the baptism. They marked the location where it was to take place. I often wondered how they were able to force two long poles into the bottom of the bayou and they stayed in place. But God was in control.

On Sunday morning, two brothers of the church and one deacon assisted the pastor with baptizing. There were about seven candidates. Catherine, Miriam, J.W and I were among them. All of us wore a large white handkerchief folded and tired around our heads. That was a tradition. I did not know what it meant because I did not ask and no one ever volunteered to explain it. We lined up across the front of the bayou to be baptized. Family members and other sisters and brothers of the church were standing around us. Someone said the first should be last and the last should be first. So, the first one to go into the water was the last one who confessed Christ. I was baptized last because I confessed Christ first. The water was warm as I waded toward the pastor who stood there with much anticipation. As

I waded toward him I told my story, "I'm *s-o glad, I got Jesus w-ay down in my soul. I told the Lord if He free my soul I'll serve Him until I die.*"

"Tell it child, tell it," Said a little old woman.

She yelled out as each candidate entered the bayou. I was baptized by Reverend Kemp and what a wonderful feeling that was! After the baptizing, the girls wore white dresses and a new white handkerchief was tied around each one's head. During the church service, the new converts sat on the front pew. Just before fellowship Mom told Miriam and I to move to another seat because we joined Mount Olive Baptist Church the 2nd Sunday. The pastor read the church covenant and the other candidates were given the right hand of fellowship. They joined New Star Baptist Church.

Women cooked and brought dinner to church in cardboard boxes. Churches did not have fellowship halls in the country. Each box was placed on the last pew in the church or on a table, which had been placed in a designated section. The congregation was served on the church grounds.

That Sunday night all the new converts sat on the same first pew, which was called the *mourner's bench*. We prayed aloud one at a time.

I got busy as a junior usher and I participated on programs at various churches in the area. Mrs. Ward is not with us today but I am thankful to God for allowing me to know her. May she rest in peace and may the legend live on!

Mount Olive Baptist Church

School

We went to school. My sisters did not have to wait until a "rainy day" to attend school as they did in Arkansas. When it was raining, we had rain gear: raincoats, umbrellas and galoshes, which are waterproof overshoes to wear. Mom made provisions for us. That is what mothers do for their children. Thank God! We were no longer in "*bondage.*"

Our echo was, "*free at last.*"
Thank God, we had been liberated. We had a chance to get a formal education. We welcomed the rain because the sandy road was our route to travel daily. When cars came into the community, we saw the dust before we saw the automobiles. If we were walking when a car passed by, our clothes were showered with sand. We thanked God for the rain because it settled the dust.

Grand Bayou Jr. High School

We lived on Marston Plantation. Our little shotgun house was up in the field so to speak. That meant we had to walk quite a distance to the road to catch the bus to ride to school. Lunch cost about 15 cents per day. Miriam was spoiled. She asked for 25 cents some days. If Papa did not give her a quarter when she asked for it, she stood beside the gate and cried. She not only cried, but also *bellowed* like a cow. She desired extra money to spend for junk. Mrs. Atkins' store and cottage was just down the road from the school. Children went there at recess or after lunch. One cent bought two banana kits or two of any kits. If a student had five cents, he could purchase ten small pieces of candy.

Ruth's Godmother, Mrs. Ophelia Toliver lived near the bus stop, but we always waited for the bus at Cousin Ella D.'s house. Strangely, snails seemed to be attracted to something there. Every morning upon arrival, I looked all around me before I put my books onto the porch. One morning there was a big snail perched on the edge of the porch. It made me sick to look at it. I was squirming and calling for somebody to put some salt on the "*thing.*" My sisters said salt would make them melt. It worked, but then the snail really looked *icky*. Wow! If it was not one thing, it was another. There were so many, many inconveniences. Nevertheless, we did not give up; we kept the faith that one-day things would change for the better! We made it through the *problematic times.*

First Grade Class @ Grand Bayou Jr. High

The school was a nice two-story building. Of course, it was formerly a school for whites only. We were thankful for the opportunity to attend there. Our books were hand-me-downs. That is, white students had used them. After they finished with them, they were given to us even if they were *ragged*. They were thought to be good enough for us.

I have some good memories of events, which took place at Grand Bayou, such as the basketball tournaments, which were held on Saturdays. We enjoyed good food and we had fun. Occasionally the school sponsored a heaven and hell party. If we chose to go to the hell party, we could have fun, dance, and be entertained with music. However, if we went to the heaven party we just communicated with the teachers, parents, and other students. Yes, we had very tasty food.

Students were not required to wear uniforms to school. However, each school had a mascot and chosen colors. Grand Bayou School colors were dark blue and gold and the mascot was a *gator*. In the 1950s, the style was can-can slips, which made the girls dresses stand out like umbrellas were underneath them. Later there was the hoop slip, which had a *ring of wire in the hem*. We thought we were looking good. The black and white oxford shoes were popular until the "*rock 'n roll*" shoes became the new style. They were also black and white but slender, or not bulky. We wore bobby socks turned down two or three times until the "*donut*" *style became popular.*

During the winter, we wore underwear called "*unions*" or "*long johns.*" The purpose was to help keep our bodies warm or shield us from the cold. The classrooms were not always comfortable, and we utilized the *radiator heaters*. Today, children have thermal underwear, which are fashioned in many colors and prints. Children and adults may wear them alike. Some of them are accessorized with ribbons to make them more attractive, but they are similar to long johns without the snaps or back flaps.

Parish & State Fair

We went to the parish fair, which was held in Coushatta and the state fair, which was held in Shreveport. The day on which blacks went to the fair was called "*dog day*." The majority of the attendees were *black*. There were displays of garments, which were fashioned by 4-H Club students. They were judged for winners. We observed livestock such as hogs, cattle and horses. There were caged chickens also. The fair was set-up for entertainment and to educate the students. Many booths were set up with delicious food, which could be purchased, and there were numerous mechanical rides such as the ferry wheel, train, carousel, bumper cars, the high swing and etc. Of course, there was a fee, but we had purchased tickets to cover the cost. I recall the "*dark room*" in which, animated ghosts were set up and as we walked through the room, the ghosts made a noise and reached out to grab us. Amazing people were there: The largest man in the world, a man who could guess one's weight and another who sketched pictures of anyone who sat before him. There was a man who handled snakes and the list goes on

Rachel @ State Fair

There were small baskets attached to the wall of a booth for anyone who chose to try his luck by pitching balls into them. The player was given three balls and if his luck was good, he won a stuffed animal. Another booth was set up with toy ducks in a stream of running water. If one chose to pick up a duck, his prize was determined by the number, which was under the duck's belly. That was usually a small stuffed animals or beads. The attractions of yesterday continue today!

Lois @ Parish Fair

Something Humorous

    All of us wore high-topped shoes to school especially in the winter. We were in elementary school then. Our *brogans* were always brown. We polished them with brown mule or ox blood polish and kept them shined. Rachel was the little one who was always doing something devilish.

"I don't like the ugly things," She complained.

One day to our surprise, she could not find her shoes. We looked high and low for them. No one could guess where they were. Rachel had tried to cut them into pieces. She put them into the *trash barrel* to be burned. Shame on Rachel!

Opportunities

While I was in school, I was a very cleaver student and eager to learn. I took part in dramatics and was involved repeatedly in spelling and math contests. I was one of the smartest students in the class and was frequently called upon to write assignments, songs, and etc. on the blackboard. We sang a song every morning and prayed the Lords' Prayer. We also repeated the Pledge of Allegiance.

It was my pleasure to recite the following in front of the class:

> The Preamble
> First Psalms
> Twenty-third Psalm
> The Gettysburg Address

I cherished the opportunity and the attention. I was so proud of myself, I wrote everything that I was told to recite. Thank God, for Mr. John Love who invented the pencil sharpener and Mr. William Purvis, the man who invented the fountain pen. We utilized Shaffer's Fountain Pens and used black or blue ink to complete homework or assignments. Math assignments were done in pencil. I graduated as valedictorian of my eight-grade class. That was an honor. Mother was exceedingly glad and she encouraged me to keep up the good work! Ruth's friends told me that I was apt. I did not even know the meaning of the word. I finally figured it out. They recognized I was quick to learn.

In Memory

Mrs. Laura Luke-Moore

Mrs. Luke was my second Grade teacher. She was an outstanding instructor. Her attire was always immaculate and her long nails were usually polished bright red. She taught me to write in cursive. I received very good grades in penmanship. That is one reason I was chosen to write on the blackboard!

I recall Mrs. Luke kept a bell, which she rang when it was time for recess and lunch break. Sometimes she appointed a student to circle the grounds while ringing the bell. After lunch, all the students lined up according to grades in front of the school. We formed nine lines because the school was a junior high. All the teachers sat on the large concrete pillars at the entrance. There were two of them. The principal spoke to us concerning activities, performance and etcetera before we were allowed to return to our respective classrooms.

8th Grade Class of 1959

My address: Our Pledge to America

We think that we are the most fortunate boys and girls in the world, for we are Americans by inheritance and because we believe in the American way of life. Americans have faith in a representative form of government. They believe that government exists for the betterment of people, that the officials are representing them and that it is the duty of such officials to work for the common good, and the general welfare of all. Americans believe that people have a right to be free and Independent.

Americans think that every person should have the right to select his own type of work, that useful and honorable work is beneficial, and that every worker is the equal of every other worker. Americans believe in freedom of thought, and freedom of speech. They believe that people have the right of choice, the choice to live and work where they wish to build their own homes, and to enjoy the rewards of their labor. They believe that people have the right to enjoy freedom in their religious life. They believe that people of this nation have a right to assemble together for peaceful purposes. They believe that citizens have a right to security of life, liberty, and the pursuit of happiness.

Americans believe in freedom not only for the people of our own United States, but for all people who desire it. They feel that it is possible to live in this air-age world side by side with other nations as neighbors, and that it is possible to carry on trade and commerce with fairness.

We are Americans, and we want to be worthy of the blessings of liberty which were guaranteed to us by our country. We want to be able to serve our country when and where we can. We know of no nation, no government which hold out so much hope, and so much promise to her citizens as does our country. We believe in our form of government and in the democratic way of life. We are proud of our American heritage and we want to be worthy.

The adults today carry on their shoulders the burden of the problems which must be solved now. It is our part to attend school; to make the most of our educational opportunities, to learn some useful trade or profession; to learn how to fix ourselves into the scheme of our national life in order that this democracy of ours may live on more gloriously and more efficiently as a leader of nations in this world. As we leave grade school, we pledge our best efforts to become worthy citizens of America, Our Heritage.

The student who was the Salutatorian had a boyfriend who was in our class. She was shy. Therefore, she did not do as well, nor did she learn her speech in a timely manner. The teacher, Mrs. Bernice Ware-Buggs had no choice but to give the speech to the next student in line. That student was Leola Foster, my friend. On the night of commencement, both of us did a great job! We were happy and our moms were very proud of us. The eighth grade class stood outside of the building and posed for a group photograph with Mrs. Bernice Ware-Buggs.

Chapter 10

The Death of a 2 Year Old

Danger Valley Plantation

The year was 1958 and I was thirteen years old.

Farming was still a way of life and there was plenty of cotton. Periodically the crops were sprayed for insects i.e., boll weevils and worms. Airplanes were utilized. All families were evacuated before the cotton was sprayed. We left the area for several hours or maybe all day. We carried food, water, other drinks and necessities. Everybody was transported to a church about five or six miles away. Most families consisted of small children. My mother had four young girls and my sister, Esther had a two-year-old girl, Precious Joy.

The spray was believed to be hazardous to one's health, perhaps deadly poison. Possibly DDT was used. It is an insecticide, which was used on crops for pest control. The three letters come from its chemical name, Dichloro-Diphenyl-Tricholoethane.

Evacuation

One morning we left home in route to the church. We were all on the plantation owner's truck like a bunch of slaves. We were packed closely *like sardines in a can*. We arrived at Mount Olive Baptist Church, the designated place on Highway 1. After waiting several hours, we returned home to find the spray still very strong. As I look back down memory lane, I recall we were riding on the truck and the smell of spray was in our nostrils. We could not help but inhale the fumes. It was in the air very strong! As we stopped in front of each house, the occupants were released to enter their dwelling place. I do not recall any instructions at that point. There were times when the cotton was sprayed and we did not leave the area. Evidently, the DDT or whatever was used that particular day was more harmful to the human race. There was no doubt about it. Esther was married and she had her own place. She lived in the house, which Mrs. Ward and family had previously lived in. The Ward family had relocated to Shreveport, Louisiana. When the truck stopped in front of Esther's house, she and Precious Joy went inside immediately. Unbelievably, the house was surrounded by cotton. I noticed a small object on the far end of the porch, but I thought nothing about it. I was young and it did not occur to me that the object was contaminated, but it was left outside exposed to the spray.

None of us could say the child did or did not retrieve the toy, which had been left outside. However, it is possible that little Precious Joy touched it, handled it, or whatever. It was left outside during the time the cotton was sprayed. Anyway, the child became very ill. Within two days, her lips had turned purple and they looked parched. She was so weak she could not stand alone and diarrhea was a problem. We did not know what was wrong, and at that time, no one suspected that her illness might have been connected to the dangerous chemical.

Plea for Help

During the night or before dawn Esther and her husband, Mr. Flames walked to get help. He had no transportation and he knew from all observations that the child was desperately in need of medical attention. They arrived at the overseer's residence. Precious Joy was still resting on his shoulder. Mr. Flames said he called out desperately several times in hopes of getting the attention of Mr. "X." He knocked and knocked on the door. It seemed as if he was being ignored. Sometimes five minutes seem like thirty. While standing there in need, Mr. Flames said little Precious Joy flinched. Life was slipping away while the *"overseer"* seemed to be unconcerned. However, we realize it was very early in the morning and just *maybe* the overseer was sound asleep. Finally, he *answered* the door but it was too late. The little one died on the shoulder of the one who tried to get help. Nothing could be done to help her at that point. She was gone but the boss allowed Mr. Flames to use his truck to carry the child to the doctor anyway. Mr. Flames said he did not tell Esther that he thought the child was gone, but I am sure she feared the worst and was in distress. She was going through a storm of *"pain and heartache."* Some things will cause a mother's heart to bleed profusely. That was one of them.

It is possible that the boss realized what had happened when he saw the child. She was unresponsive. She was carried to Coushatta, Louisiana, which was twelve miles away. That is where the nearest doctor practiced. After a number of hours, Esther returned to Mother's house but without her little girl. It was still early that morning when the truck neared our house. I could see my sister waving her hands up and down. She was crying uncontrollably. We knew something had happened. Nevertheless, we did not think Precious Joy was gone! We were shocked when we were told the news.

Questionable Death

An autopsy was performed. We were told the marrow; vascular tissue in the interior cavities of her bones had dried up. We were not given any possible reasons why and I never understood it. I wondered, "How was that and were we told the whole truth? Were the facts concealed?" How sad and what a tragedy. The little one's life had just begun, but she suddenly left her earthly family and went home to be with the Lord.

Overseer's Residence, the big house

There was no investigation to my knowledge. Esther contacted our dad to ask if he would help her in some way. He came at her request only to ask what happened. We needed him to help us find the answer to that very same question. He did nothing and we were right back to point "A." I wondered why an attorney was not hired to investigate the tragedy. We did not have any money, but that should have been a concern of mean Pharaoh's. He should have known how to handle it. He was always scrambling for money. I thought he would have pursued the matter in court in order to get the answers, which we desperately needed. Nothing could have brought the child back, but someone should have taken the responsibility for what happened. That is, had it been proven that Precious Joy died because of exposure to a deadly chemical. The family believes the child's death was connected to the insecticide.

Precious Joy was buried in Grand Bayou, Louisiana. She was laid to rest between our maternal grandmother and a distant relative of her father. On that same day, my sister returned to the gravesite to pray. She said she had to do that while the body of her little angel was still there. Esther was burdened down under the weight of the little girl's death. It was not strange that she kneeled down to pray at the gravesite. It was the perfect time and place to give her burden to the Lord. She knew she could not bring the child back.

Surely, Esther felt a sense of relief. She knew the child went to be with the Lord. Precious Joy was just a little angel and I believe the Master had need of her. We do not understand the ways of our Lord, for His ways are higher than our ways. Neither are we to question his judgments. Christ claimed his own and all of us wondered why because our hearts were broken with grief. Those who have not experienced the loss of a child cannot completely identify. Surely, we have some idea but until it hits home we will not really know the hurt.

David's first son by Bath-sheba was very sick. David besought God for the child and he fasted. Scripture tells us on the seventh day the child died. David went into the house of the Lord and worshiped, then he came to his own house and he did eat. David knew that he could not bring the child back. However, there is something that we can do when burdened. We can give it to the Lord. He is a heavy load bearer and He *is* able to sustain us. The Lord is our everything.

After the tragedy, the other children were carried to the doctor to be checked, examined, etc. It seemed as if someone knew something that was not being told. If there was no suspicion or proof, there was no need to require medical examinations for the other children. Mother did not request the exams. I never heard her say she paid one red cent for the medical examinations. She never mentioned an itemized bill at all. It was very difficult to explain what was going on to the children. We did not know ourselves. There were a multitude of unanswered questions and everybody seemed to be *tight-lipped*. Esther soon purchased a headstone for little Precious Joy's grave.

"Papa taught me that we should place headstones on the graves of our love ones," She stated.

We returned to the site repeatedly while trying to readjust. Many times, we went there to clean the site. There were many dark days in our lives. One may liken them to *tornados* with gusty winds, which forced us into a valley of despair. I am reminded that no storm can take us where the grace and mercy of God cannot find us.

David said, *if I ascend up into heaven, thou art there: if I make my bed in hell, behold, thou art there.*

Psalm 139:8 (KJV)

Precious Joy
Born: 6-21-1956
Died: 8-10-1958

Chapter 11

Growing Up

I was forced to assume responsibilities early in life because Mother was not well. She had been ill for some time and she was given an injection every month. She had a heart problem. I learned about it after my baby sister was born. I did not know how serious it was. Mother walked quite a distance to the bus stop at Abington Road and Highway 1. A little store was on the corner. She waited there to board the bus. When she noticed the bus approaching she walked out into the highway and used a large white handkerchief to flag it down. She went to Confederate Memorial Hospital for her treatments. Before she returned home, she purchased something from H. L. Green Department Store for us. She bought little handkerchiefs, which had cartoon characters on them or coconut hut candy. She bought socks or whatever she could afford to buy from J.C. Penny. She loved her children and we loved her.

Maturity

By the time I was eighth grade, I was beginning to develop into a young woman. My classmates always teased me until I was embarrassed. All the other girls were larger and well developed. Perhaps that is the reason one of my uncles called me *"peanut."* I was tiny. By the time that I was tenth grade, I was a little more mature but very shy.

I had a Godmother. Even though she did not have much, she shared her resources with me. I was excited to receive packages through the mail.

Godmother always wrapped the bundles securely and I opened them with much anticipation. As I removed the ties, my younger sisters gathered beside me. Their little faces were all aglow as if it were Christmas. I received items of clothing and I was appreciative. They were hand-me-downs but I added them to my wardrobe. I wore them with pride because they were new to me.

We had moved into one of several little houses, which were very close to the highway. I called the section, Borden's Quarters. On Sundays, we attended Sunday school and church services were great. Sometimes in the evenings, I was a little depressed; bored almost to tears because I was lonely. I tried to do something to occupy my time. I played jacks, connect the dots, tic-tac-toe, and sometimes I walked to the corner of Wilson Road and Highway 1 and sat on the grass. We had no transportation, but while watching the cars come and go it occurred to me, one day I will have my own car.

Esther and Mr. Flames relocated to the same area, but they lived closer to the corner store. They had four children and Esther worked for the Colemans. Mr. Flames did odd jobs. Mother sent Anna or Lois to baby sit and prepare breakfast for the children. Since jobs were scarce, Esther's husband decided to seek employment in Shreveport. He lived there but returned home on weekends to bring groceries for his family. That did not last long. Mr. Flames seemed to disappear off the face of the earth. He left his family behind. That was a *storm of desertion*. Their youngest child was a baby.

Each house had its own aluminum water tank. We did not have to pump water to take care of our needs. We no longer cut wood to burn because we had a butane tank. That was a blessing. Each house had a little outhouse in the rear. Actually, each house was moved from another location into a pasture. That's were we lived. A barbed wire fence was in front of the houses. Someone used a grass sack to pull the wires apart making an opening, which allowed us easy access to the road. We held our dresses between our legs to avoid a tare. One day we returned home from school and the wire fence had been removed. We were happy!

We loved our new location because Mother no longer walked several miles to catch a bus in route to the hospital. The school bus came right by our house also, and Wilson Lake was just down the road from where we lived. That was a popular place to fish.

Outhouses & basketball goal in rear

My first cousins, the Taylors lived next door to us. They moved from the plantation too. After Papa was stricken with a stroke, he lost his sight. The job was a bit much for Mom's nieces and nephew to handle. They were still in school too. Mom took care of business for Papa. She was the caretaker for her father and her sister for many years. Auntie was hospitalized several times. Her stay was always lengthy. Mother and Papa went to visit with her many times before he lost his sight. Finally, Auntie came home for good and we were happy for her.

My two cousins had boyfriends who came by on Sunday evenings. They were not serious, but I did not have a close friend. I had no boyfriend at age 16. Therefore, no one came to visit me.

"That's good and maybe I should go to the convent and become a Nun," I thought.

"But what kind of life does a Nun have?,"I began to rethink that idea.

I never thought of dropping out of school because I loved it and always wanted to do something to prosper. On *"may day"* or *"field day"* in 1961, I met Romeo. He was a charming little fellow with big eyes and naturally pretty hair. We rode to school on the same bus and sometimes we sat together especially, in the evenings. One evening while in conversation and not paying attention to the time, he caused us to miss the school bus going home. We rode with his friend, Freeman who drove his sports car behind the bus. Some of the students laughed and waved to me but I was embarrassed. I knew that was another reason for associates to tease me. Romeo and I became close friends. He graduated from high school one year before I did. Later, he went to the United States Army. We exchanged many letters and photos while he was stationed at Fort Polk, Louisiana. At Christmas, he bought a gift for me and one for my mom. I thought that was sweet and very generous of him. Romeo loved my mother because she was so mild-mannered.

Even though Mom spoke softly, she meant what she said, "Keep your dress down and hold yourself up."

I understood what she meant because I had heard it many times before. Today parents formulate that same statement differently.

Generally speaking, "Do not become sexually involved. Do not put yourself in *danger of becoming pregnant and jeopardize your education. Furthermore, you do not need a baby while you are young and unmarried. That will bring about problems for all involved.*" That was a lecture or a sermonette. When I was a little girl, I heard grown-ups talk about girls who were pregnant.

"That girl broke her leg," They said.

I could not understand what they meant by such a statement. The girl did not seem to have a problem walking. There was no cast on her leg, and neither was she using crutches. As time passed, the girl grew in size and her dress code changed. She did not wear the tight dresses anymore. Her style changed to maternity wear or tent style dresses. I heard discussions about her weird cravings. She had an appetite for clay dirt, pickles with peppermint candy, and chocolate cake.

"There is plenty of clay dirt down by the levee, "Mother said to Cousin Ella D.
"Yeah, Mamie told me," She acknowledged that she already knew.
"She said that's where she found a plenty clay dirt," Cousin continued.

As I grew up, I thought about the statement, which grown-ups made about the girl who *broke her leg*. I wondered what our elders meant. Then it clicked! The hymen is a thin mucous membrane that completely covers the opening of the vagina. That is what they meant! *I figured it out.* Perhaps, they were being respectful by talking over our heads. They were also keeping us in the dark. However, I still cannot understand why women ate clay dirt.

Regardless of what happen, or did not happen, I can never say too much about my mom! Even though Aunt Matt could not read nor write, Mom wrote letters to her quite often. In the early 60's the cost of stamps was 4 cents each. Most times Mom bought stamped envelopes. Today they seem to have become obsolete and this generation knows nothing about them. However, Auntie's neighbors were very good to her. They were kind enough to read Mom's letters for her hearing. With that thought in mind, I chose to share one of Mom's last letters with the readers of this book. I have some of Auntie's possessions and several letters are among them. They are priceless keepsakes.

Letter from Mom to Aunt Mattie

Preparation for Graduation in 1963

We had two 12th Grade homeroom teachers. They were Mrs. Mansfield and Mrs. Hollywood. Mr. A. Headmaster was the school principal. Apparently, they chose the top seven honor students according to (GPA) grade point averages. Only a few points separated each student's GPA. Those students were #1- Henry Miles, 2nd- Major Tillman, 3rd- Jane Thorne, 4th- Hannah Turner, 5th-Alice Mason, 6th Gayle Barnes and 7th- Laura Mann. The top four students earned a right to speak during the commencement exercises, which were held on Thursday evening, May 30, nineteen hundred sixty-three. The teachers agreed to give the fourth speech to Gayle Barnes. They looked all over me with no concern as if I did not exist. They skipped over the fifth graduate also. I wanted to know why I was not given the opportunity to exercise my right. No one could say that I was not capable; neither could one say I did not earn that right. In fact, no one explained anything to me.

Some of the students speculated, "Gayle Barnes participated in dramatics and the teachers like her. That's why you didn't get your speech."

Perhaps that was true, but the teachers should have had the common courtesy to say, "We think Gayle Barnes is the better choice." Of course, that was too much like right. I was hurt and I knew what they did was not fair. I went home and told Mom about the underhanded favor.

"You are graduating so don't worry about it," Said Mom.
"I know you can speak because you spoke well when you graduated from 8th grade as Valedictorian," She continued.

All of that was true but it was also beside the point. Sometimes I thought Mom was too passive. Nothing justified the teachers' actions. They were prejudiced; they had their favorites in those days just as some prefer one to another today. They had respect of persons and chose *not* to give honor to whom honor was due. Mr. Headmaster was the principal and he read the names of the top students to the class. He was aware of their little dirty deed and he allowed such an injustice to take place. Thus, he was as guilty as the two instructors were.

"Ok, they are in charge, but I was told every dog has a day and a good dog has two, I recalled."

Class Day

Some of the students prepared a program. The committee made a will from the 12th grade class. Many students were angry and their feelings were hurt. I recall the will stated, "Hannah Turner wills her glorious hair to short hair Mary." The student confronted me and made derogatory statements. I assured her that I had nothing to do with the writing of the will and neither was I aware of its contents. To say the least, she was furious! However, her hair was micro-short. O' well!, she got over the statement. She was angry with the wrong person.

When I graduated from high school, Romeo was in Germany and could not come to the ceremony. I was very proud of myself, 4th honor student at Southside High School. The class was small and approximately forty-five students graduated. There were a few who dropped out of school. My mother was happy especially because I was the first of seven girls to graduate. Unbelievable, my dad came to the graduation. He surprised me! I had sent him an invitation but I did not know if he were coming.

Grambling College

In the fall of 1963, I enrolled as a student at Grambling College. Thank God for my loving mother and Mr. P. L. Buggs, Principal of Grand Bayou Jr. High School. Mr. Buggs helped me get started and I was so excited. Before then, I did not think I would be able to go to college due to financial reasons. Mom borrowed $100.00 dollars for me. She helped me get the necessary things together. Mr. Buggs loaded my belongings into his automobile, and we went to Grambling. While there, I worked in the laboratory school library to earn part of my tuition. That was arranged by Mr. Buggs, who had connections with people who were in authoritative positions. Many advance today because of whom they know!

The disappointing part about going to college was the fact that I was not able to obtain a "*loan*" from The Upscale Bank. I tried unsuccessfully. Perhaps I should have tried again with another bank, but I did not have that opportunity. Dad lived in Shreveport but he did not volunteer to apply for a bank loan for me. Neither did he say he would take me to inquire about one for myself. There were no grants at that time to my knowledge or, possibly, there were, but they were not available to our race. Usually, we are last to be considered for anything that is worthwhile or rewarding.

When a student is recognized, he has demonstrated remarkable skills, which cannot be ignored. A new day is dawning!

In the spring of 1964, I wanted to return to school, but I did not have any money. I could not earn enough by working in the library. I asked Dad if he would help me. He borrowed $100.02 for me. The fall semester was a difficult time for me. I had no options except to adjust to being away from home. In addition to everything else, Mother was not well. I was concerned about her health. Therefore, we kept in touch by writing letters. No! We did not have a telephone, even in 1964.

I had a wonderful roommate, Patti. I was able to discuss many subject matters with her. Patti was from Baton Rouge, Louisiana and her father was a minister. He was ill also. We had some things in common and therefore, we could relate concerning certain topics.

I had begun to adjusted and felt more comfortable about being away from my immediate family. Then my roommate's father passed away. That was much to deal with and it certainly did not make things any better for me. There were *storms of heartaches* in both of our lives. We endeavored to stand up against the pressure, which virtually beat us down. We were both old enough to know that God's will must be done and we struggled to be strong. Patti had the assurance that her father had gone to a better place even though she loved him; they were separated by "*death.*"

I spoke seriously to Patti. I recalled, Luke tells us there is a "*great gulf*" fixed. Read the passage of scripture about Lazarus and the rich man Luke 16: 19-31 (KJV). It is a revelation! At the end of the semester, Patti and I went our separate ways and we never saw each other again.

Romeo and I continued to exchange letters and photos. He told me that he wanted to get married. Next, I received a set of wedding rings by mail. We were in love or, I thought that he loved me. Some people say children have "*puppy love.*" Well, even a puppy has feelings. That is something to take under consideration. Anyway, I placed the ring on my finger and just admired it for a little while. My mind was traveling literally and I had one thought after another. Finally, I placed the ring back into the box from whence it came and stored it away. For a few minutes, my mind was taken away from the worry, which was at hand. At that time, I had not been told, if you are going to worry, do not pray and if you pray, do not worry. Well, I was worried. Mother's birthday was July 19 and she really was not well. She had a birthday party. That was the first that I had known her to have, and it was her last party. She made the decision and planned it herself. I believe she knew that her life was nearing an end.

Fall 1964

Again, I did not have any money to pay my tuition and consequently I was not able to return to college. Mom was ill and I did not dare ask her to borrow money for me again. Anyway, I was needed at home. Mother was hospitalized frequently. She told me the doctor stated that she had a benign tumor. Apparently, that was not true. She was very ill and she was hospitalized for heart catheterization. She went home for a short period then returned to the hospital for surgery. Mother was there a number of weeks. I went by continental trail way bus to visit with her many times. One day I went to the bus stop and I waited, and waited for the bus. Finally, it arrived. It was delayed for some reason. Nevertheless, I boarded it and came to Shreveport. I walked from the bus station to the corner of Texas Street at H. L. Green Store. I boarded the trolley. By the way, Mr. Elbert R. Robinson invented the electric trolley. He deserved recognition. We travel in comfort and take many things for granted, but thank God for a skillful man, Mr. Robinson.

Mom's Medical Condition

I went to Confederate Memorial Hospital and when I arrived, visiting hour was over. During that time visitors were required to stop at the desk to receive a pass card before proceeding to the wards to visit with the patients. Two cards were filed for each patient and if both cards had been given out, you were out of luck. You did not visit with your relative, friend, or acquaintance. There was a mean gray-haired Caucasian woman at the desk. She walked with a limp. Her attitude was unbecoming to describe it at best. She would not permit me to visit even though I had come from out-of-town. It did not matter to her how far I had come or why I was late. I know she was an employee and she was expected to follow rules. However, she could have spoken with compassion. She was very ugly, prejudiced, mean, and hateful. She was always unprofessional, even on other occasions. Perhaps she had a stony heart and a troubled spirit, and all of that could have been changed had she chosen to amend her ways.

I was very disturbed as I boarded the trolley, returned to the bus station, and waited for the next trail way to ride back home without seeing my mother. I did not know my way around in the hospital. Therefore, I did not know how to take an alternate route to get to the floor where my mother was. I had gone 37 miles only to be disappointed. I spent money for a blank trip. Some time later, I informed Ruth about what happened.

"If I go to visit and there are no cards available, I walk up the stairs to second floor, She said.

If I am questioned, I tell them I am going to donate blood," She continued as if that was ok.
I did not know to do that, and I am not sure that I would have tried it anyway. I prefer to follow rules, but Mom was sick and I really wanted to see her! I really did!

Mom had a very serious operation. She said the doctor told her she would not have to go through menopause if she had the surgery. Thereby, she would avoid the problems, which are associated with the *"change of life."* Naturally, he did tell her that. Mother had radiation treatments also. Shortly thereafter, she was confronted with other problems and the doctor informed her that she needed another operation. I was young at that time and I had no medical knowledge of such surgery. So much was done within a short period. I really did not understand it. After all of the surgery, Mother only became weaker and weaker. The last time Mother returned home from the hospital she did not stop until after she had gone next door to see her father. I do not know the details of their conversation, but I believe Mom explained her condition and her final decision to her dad.

While Mom was home, she talked with us about staying together. My oldest sister was instructed to take care of us until we were able to care for ourselves. Perhaps there were other reasons for her to take on more responsibilities also. God knows what lies ahead. He knows the contents of our hearts, and He knows where all the pitfalls are. This may have been good for Ruth. However, looking at the situation from a carnal point of view, it seemed to be too much for the young woman. Now I recall, *"All things work together for good..."*

I recall what Jesus said to John from the cross. *When Jesus therefore saw his mother, and the disciple standing by, whom he loved, he saith unto his mother,*

Woman, behold thy son! Then saith he to the disciple, Behold thy mother! And from that hour that disciple took her unto his own home.

John 19:26-27(KJV)

I recognize that John, the beloved disciple was instructed to look after the mother of Jesus. These instructions were given shortly before Jesus bowed his head and gave up the ghost.

As I continue to reminisce, I recall something else.

"Don't you'll forget about me," Mom said in a quiet but serious voice.

She was really saying, "Remember me. I took care of you and gave you the best that I could provide. I taught you to give God thanks for each day. Remember the good things which I did for all of you."

"I prayed and asked the Lord to take me," She said a few minutes later.

She was sick, tired of suffering, and ready to go home. She had prepared to go to Heaven, a prepared place for prepared people. Mother had given me a 5x7-color photograph. She told me to place it on my dresser after I get married. She thought I would have married Romeo. Although I did not marry my high school fiancé, the photo is *on my dresser*. The last birthday card, which Mother gave to me is also among my possessions. I cherish them.

Mother was terminally ill and I felt so helpless. I did not know what to do as she spoke to us, and it was as if God had warned her. Maybe she had a glimpse of heaven. Many times, I tried to focus my attention on something pleasant, but nothing removed the thought of death from my wondering mind. I was going through a gloomy *storm of disappointment, sadness, and pain.* I came face to face with despair, although I was familiar with it because I had been there before. Sometimes I wore my engagement ring and I longed for my dear friend to come home, but he was so far away. Mother was hospitalized again. Ruth had her own apartment in Shreveport. She had three young children who lived with Mother before she became so terribly ill. Mother had told Ruth that she was not able to keep her children any longer. I went to live with Ruth. I left my younger sisters with Esther. I was Ruth's baby sitter during the day while she worked, and I had the opportunity to visit with our mother too. We took turns visiting with Mother while she was hospitalized. The last time I saw her alive she told me her feet were so cold, and they were. I recall some of the nurses' aides were repulsive and I shall never forget what Mother told me.

"They treat you so bad," She said in a soft tone.
"Especially if you are by yourself," She said sadly.

That was hard to hear from Mom who was slowly slipping away. No one should be cruel to a helpless patient, but some employees show up to get a paycheck and not to work. They seem to have no conscience. Healthcare workers should be caring people.

"Payday is coming after a while," Grandfather said many times.
"When you're hurt, you did it yourself," He said.

On Mom's face was a different expression and I wanted to ask her something but I was afraid. I did not know just how to formulate my question, so I remained silent. Possibly, I would have asked the wrong question. In addition, I did not know if I would have dealt with her answer without becoming emotional. I returned to my sister's place deeply disturbed. In my mind, I heard the song, *"God will take care of you."* I did not know it was penned by William Harfield, a blind preacher who had no one to care for him but friends. He put his trust in God. I had to do the same.

Ruth went to the hospital that evening and she returned about 3:00 a.m. along with our cousin whose name was Ruth also. As I opened the door and saw the look on her face, I knew something was wrong. Her first statement to me was Mother "dear" is dead. I was speechless and I sat down and wept. I quickly remembered the look on Mother's face when I saw her the last time. I was afraid of what seemed to be happening. Now, I know she was slowly passing away. I knew it was coming, but I was not ready for it. How does one get ready for the death of a loved one? Mother passed away on March 16, 1965 at the age of 42. She was still a young woman. I had just turned twenty years old in January. I was very sorry that cancer had claimed my mother's life. I cannot begin to tell how sad I was. Mrs. Elaine Marks carried Ruth and me to Grand Bayou to tell the children our mom was gone. Her pain and suffering was over. She left us in the hands of the Lord. As I looked back over my life, which was filled with a multitude of heartaches, I realized I had become motherless. There were four children who were younger than I was. My baby sister was just *nine* years old. As I looked even further down that long and narrow pathway which contains so many twists and turns, I quickly formed a mental picture of my mother as she struggled to take care of us. She had seven girls and I endeavored to make a difference. I desired to graduate from college, secure a job, and set an example worthy of emulation for my younger sisters. Suddenly, my dream was over shadowed. I could not adequately express my sorrow.

Two Deaths within 24 hrs.

March 17, 1965 my mother's father passed away only hours after her death. Cousin Ella D. was at Papa's house. She knew the children needed help. She sat in the room beside Papa's bed.

"Cousin Ella D. said, y'all come on," Rachel said to me.

"Papa was passing away as we entered his room, then Samuel went with me to alert the land lady," She said.

"It was around 3.00 a.m.," Rachel continued.

"It was dark and I was so scared," Rachel said.

What a hardship that was! No, it was not a shock, but we were not ready for such an announcement. My mother and her father were both very ill and sad, but we hated to see them go. They left the land of *pain and suffering*. Mother did not have to bear the hardship of being *mistreated* anymore.

They were healed because the spirit lifts when the Lord says, *"well done."* Mr. P.L. Buggs carried Ruth, Rachel, and Miriam to Jenkins' Funeral Home in Mansfield, Louisiana. He knew we did not have transportation. They arranged to bury Mother and her father.

I really did need a friend. Surprisingly, Romeo came home from Germany and he was a very understanding friend. I was just amazed at the fact that he came home at that particular time. Surely, God was in the plan. All that I could think of was the fact that my mother was gone! It was as if something pierced my heart and caused it to bleed profusely leaving me without strength.

On March 21, 1965, I sat in a car at the church waiting for the arrival of my mother's body and her dad's.

"Here they come," Said Romeo while looking down the highway.

"Hum, hum, hum," I moaned, as I looked to see the hearses approaching the church.

"Turn around," Said Romeo, while trying to block my view.
He kept trying to talk with me, but my heart felt like it was sinking. I could not hold back the tears. Two black hearses rolled up in front of the church. They were carrying two bodies. My heart began to pound like a hammer working overtime. There were a pink pastel casket and a light blue casket.

Memorial service was held for both family members at Mount Olive Baptist Church, Grand Bayou, Louisiana on Sunday, March 21 at one-thirty p.m. The church was filled to capacity and people were standing in the doorway and outside as well. The choir sang, "In the Sweet By and By" as we walked quietly into the sanctuary. Reverend Murphy Giles read Scriptures. Reverend Percy Sharp prayed the prayer of consolation. The choir followed with a familiar song, *"Near the Cross."* Several deacons spoke and Mrs. Ward sang a solo. Deacon will Upshaw sang Papa favorite hymn, *"Shine on me."* Reverend L.C. Kessee was asked to do the eulogies and Reverend Henry followed with the oration. Reverend G.W. Holmes, Pastor, made remarks. Mother and her father were laid to rest in New Star Cemetery.

It seemed as if the world had come to an abrupt end. It was extremely hard for all of us and perhaps the most difficult time of our lives. I realized others had traveled the same road but that did not make it easier. However, Mrs. Mary Francis, my fourth grade teacher was by my side. She really tried to comfort me.

"I lost my mother too," She said, while wiping tears from her eyes. Thereby, she reminded me that she had also walked the same dark and dreary pathway. She could identify with me and she felt my pain. Mother had styled her hair and her daughter's many times.

Reflecting on the life of Job

And there were born unto *him seven sons and three daughters.* (Job 1:2) *...Thy sons and thy daughters were eating and drinking wine in their eldest brothers house: and behold, there came a great wind from the wilderness, and smote the four corners of the house, and it fell upon the young men and they are dead....*

Job 1: 18-19 (KJV)

115

After Job received the news, scripture tells me that he arose and rent his mantle and shaved his head and fell down upon the ground and worshiped. He was faced the death of *multiple family members* at the same time.

During our time of sorrow, many people did nice things for us. They were very compassionate and yet, there was a void in our lives, which could not be filled with material things. Mrs. Viola Powell-Nash went to A&P Grocery Store in Shreveport and purchased food for us. Support from Grand Bayou Faculty was overwhelming.

"God took two soldiers at one time," Said Cousin Mamie.

I understand what she meant and I know God can do whatever He wants to, when He wants to. God is omnipotent! He took both my mother and her dad within hours. We grieved the lost of both at the same time. I believe it is well with their souls and the echo of both is the words of Paul: *I have fought a good fight, I have finished my course, I have kept the faith: Henceforth there is   laid up for me a crown of righteousness which the Lord, the righteous judge, shall give to me at that day: and not to me only, but unto all them that love his appearing.*

II Timothy 4:7-8 (KJV)

I found comfort in that passage of scripture and I knew to look to the Lord from whence cometh my help. However, during my time of sorrow it seemed as though I could not see my way. That was from a carnal point of view. I was in a storm; I was being tossed about by strong winds. They just kept on *blowing* and I kept struggling to stay on my feet. Thank God for his grace and mercy! Thank God for his Word! I was able to stroll through the computer of my mind and find help, hope, and assurance. I remembered the scripture that says, *"I am with you always, even unto the end of the world."* I knew I was not alone and there was no need to be afraid. Nevertheless, when low in spirit, fear will creep in. However, I observed, *"hope"* with great expectations. I felt *"help"* to relieve distress and I heard *"assurance"* that everything was all right. *Fear thou not; for I am with thee: be not dismayed; for I am Thy God: I will strengthen thee; yea, I will help thee; yea, I will uphold thee with the right hand of my righteousness.*

Isaiah 41:10 (KJV)

I was the oldest one at home so I played the role of Mom and I even slept in her bed. I had four young sisters to care for. I must say I did my very best to send them to school dressed decently. I combed their hair neatly and I did my daily chores. In the evenings, we did homework together. A very good friend, Celia came and spent the night with me numerous times. She was good company and she felt my pain!

First Residence in Shreveport

Family Relocated

It was not long before we moved to Shreveport with my big sister. We had assistance from Romeo who helped us relocate when he came to Grand Bayou in his truck. The new address was in the 1500 block of West 58th Street. We even had a telephone, although it was connected to a party line. We could pick up the receiver and hear our party in conversation.

While living on West 58th Street, I experienced something terrible. Mr. Lee Strong, a tall husky man who was an insurance salesperson came to our house. He was not a stranger, but a well-known public figure. I was the only one home at the time. Ruth had placed money inside the receipt book to pay the life insurance premium. I knew Mr. Strong had come to collect the payment. I gave the booklet to him and he wrote the amount paid and returned it to me. Then he quickly grabbed me around my little waist and pulled me close to him. He fondled my breast and I fought him by pushing and bumping him with my knee. He ignored my weak rejection, which, evidently was of no effect. He tried to kiss me and I jumped up and down on his feet.

"Stop it, let me go," I cried, while shoving him away from me. I pushed him with all my strength.

He finally backed off and left the house in haste. I was very disturbed because of his actions. As soon as Ruth returned home, I ran to her and explained what Mr. Strong had done to me.

"He's a man," She said to me.
"What are you saying," I asked with a loud voice.

Ruth did not answer. In other words, that could be expected not only from him but from other men as well. I was so hurt I went into the bedroom and cried. I had always looked to Ruth for protection and I really expected her to do something! After I looked back and consider the incident, I realized I could have reported it myself, since Ruth took it lightly. I was let down by my own sister. I would have never believed she would be nonchalant about my safety. I had no one else to turn to.

Mrs. Marshall Lee Hall was one of the teachers who taught at Grand Bayou Jr. High School. She lived on Nicholson Street in Shreveport. We were fortunate to receive assistance from her. She picked the girls up at our house and carried them to school every day for about six weeks. Because of Mrs. Hall's support, the girls did not have to enroll in school in Shreveport until the fall semester of 1965. May God bless her soul and may she rest in peace.

The children attended Hollywood Elementary; the principal was Mrs. G. V. Cole. After about a year, we moved to 5846 Ledbetter Street. We had more square footage at that location, and we lived close to Calvary Baptist Church. Reverend Richard Kessee was the pastor. We attended service there because it was convenient. We knew the pastor before we relocated and we went to school with some of his children.

In Memory

Mrs. Marshall Lee Hall

The Big Shock

Shortly after moving to Ledbetter Street my best friend, Romeo became involved with someone else. He was stabbed while visiting his new female associate and in the company of Sir John. He was transported to Confederate Memorial Medical Center where he underwent surgery and miraculously recovered. I went to visit him. He came by my sister's house to talk with me after he was discharged and well enough to drive. He refused to acknowledge that he had made a mistake. There were other problems

119

with our relationship also. He had baggage, which he denied. We resolved our friendship because of his actions. Days later, he called me concerning his rings. I finally returned them to him and we went our separate way.

I had always worked to help make ends meet. Such jobs were elevator operator at Palais Royal Department Store. During the Christmas holidays, I wrapped gifts at Woolworth Department Store. I was also a babysitter and nurse's aide at Gowen's Sanitarium on Line Avenue. I operated an elevator at Washington Youree Hotel also. I saw more than I can ever explain! Captain Shreve Hotel was next door and there was much traffic through the two hotels. I did not earn very much money but I was thankful. I learned early in life to thank God for whatever I have. I retained the lessons, which Mom taught me. In other words, be conservative and take care of what you have.

Rachel lived with us on Ledbetter Street a short period. She worked a job and looked for a house for her family. They relocated to Shreveport months later. Rachel and I shopped at Spartan's Atlantic Store. It was located where Women and Children's Clinic is today on Kings Highway. Spartan's was an inexpensive store. That is why we chose to shop there. Occasionally, we rode the trolley downtown to shop at Hearne's Department Store. The managers / salespersons were very prejudiced. They did not allow "*black people*" to try on clothes. If you wanted to purchase a dress, you had to know your exact size or look at the garment and assume that it was your correct size. If you bought it, you could not return it under any circumstances! If you made a mistake or used poor judgment, you suffered the consequences, *a storm of disappointment* to say the least!

Esther relocated to Shreveport. She did not want to be left behind either. She lived in King Court #2 just across Hollywood Avenue. Her little residence was within walking distance from Ruth's place.

We bought groceries from Piggy-Wiggly Store and Kroger Groceries. Gipson's Store was located beside Kroger. We walked to those stores, but we had to place our groceries in double bags. We collected Top Value stamps and S&H green stamps. We filled booklets with them and we had a catalog to decide which items we wanted to purchase. The Redemption Store was located on Southern Avenue.

One morning I decided to walk to the nearest convenient store on Hollywood Avenue to purchase a few items for myself. I was not gone very long before our neighbor's son went into our house and stole my class ring. Apparently, he was looking for money. He saw me leave the house. The truth is, we were as poor as he and his family were, or poorer. I knew he had taken my ring, which was on the dresser in my bedroom. I went next door immediately, and demanded him to give me my class ring. He slowly pulled it out of the pocket of his blue jean.

"Thank you and don't ever do that again," I said in a firm voice.

One day our neighbor was discussing our living arrangements and other business as if it were her own. A woman who many thought to be a friend to my sister decided to give her a bit of advice. She told Ruth, "*I would put her (me) out.*" I was not the problem. Perhaps I was considered to be grown or an adult. My sister had been ill and under a tremendous amount of stress. She had also been hospitalized for surgery and she needed by assistance. Ruth did not need to hear the negative advice from the naysayer. Her friend Mr. Short Stuff did not make matters better. In fact, he added fuel to the fire, which was already blazing high. He threw his weight around many times and one thing led to another. I reminded him of a few facts: *He was nobody's father there and neither was he taking care of anybody there.* That was considered grounds for dismissal, which had already been discussed. I was also told that I killed our mom by asking her to borrow $100.00 to put me in school. That really hurt me, but I knew it was not true. Mom wanted to see me in school! At least I was trying to advance.

My orders were to *move out* and get my own life insurance. That was ugly and it was said very ugly! But God made a way!

One day Ruth was resting in bed. She said something that did not make any sense to me. I puzzled my brain trying to determine what she meant.

Mr. Short Stuff stood there looking crazy.
"I doubt that she'll ever snap out of it," He quipped.
"What do you consider it to be?," I asked not really expecting an answer from him.
Mr. Short Stuff continued to stand there and ignore me. It was possible that he was part of the problem. I was glad when he left. As if that was not enough, Pharaoh called.

"I'm sending y'all some money and you save $10.00 for me," He said angrily. I cashed the check and gave the money to Ruth. Pharaoh showed up a couple of days later.

"Whar' my money?," He asked as if he had really done something.

"I gave it to Ruth, and you should not have sent it if you want it back," I said, as if I were in charge.

Somebody needed to speak up. Dad was furious with me. He had not changed but was still the hard-hearted person whom I had always known him to be. He called me a *smart cookie*! He got into his car and left driving as if he were on the freeway! He was mad!

Meager Pay

My little salary was only twenty-three dollars per week and part of that was used for bus fare. On Sundays, I walked to work from Ledbetter Street to Line Avenue, which took approximately an hour and a half or longer. I did it in order to save money and because the trolley service was very slow. I had always sacrificed in one way or another. I also did things to help others, which sometimes resulted in me having the short end of the stick. In spite of everything, I moved out reluctantly. I did get myself some life insurance like Ruth told me to do. I could only pay a premium for a $500.00 policy. That was not enough, but it was all I could afford. I sacrificed to pay the small premium. It was a twenty-year policy.

I did not have any furniture neither did I have money to buy any. I had bought a little pink wastebasket from H. L. Green. I purchased a set of dishes, which I placed on lay-a-way at Dale's Jewelers. That is all I had in addition to my clothes. I already knew what hard times were like. I had not forgotten my past in Wilson, Arkansas. I moved across town to 1446 Hard Knocks Street. The house was very big and an old one at that. It consisted of three apartments. The furniture was very old. The first tenants were a woman and her husband. They had several children. To my surprise, I had gone to school with the woman, but she was older than I was. There was also the second tenant, an older woman who became upset if one did not speak to her in the same manner in which she spoke to them. If she said hello, she expected a "*hello*" in response not, "*how are you?*" The third apartment section was for me. It was big and ragged. I was afraid to live alone so I prayed that God would send me a roommate. I was not ready to live by myself. A woman came by and asked to share the apartment with me. Her name was Jackie. She was a complete stranger to me, and I was even more afraid because I did not know what type of person she was.

"God is she my roommate?," I asked.

Well, she stayed a few weeks before a man came to move her out. He said that he was her husband. The man started looking through our belongings.

"Those are my things," I interrupted.
"I know Jackie's things; she don't fold nothing," He remarked as if he knew her well.

After that, I did not say anything else. I decided to observe. After he gathered all of Jackie's possessions, he left. Apparently, she was not my roommate. Another woman asked to share the apartment after Jackie moved out. Her name was Jezebel. She was employed at Gown's Sanitarium also. I felt better about her living with me, but she turned out to be a very rowdy person who had a lot of male company. Therefore, I was still afraid.

Suddenly my thoughts were about my younger sisters. I wondered, "How are they doing?" I had always shown concern by helping at home. I wanted to go see the children but I did not want to go empty handed. Although I was thrown out of the house, I considered that to be a test of my strength. Just maybe the devil meant it for bad, but God meant it for my good. After all was said and done, I was not bitter. Even though funds were scarce, I decided to count my little coins in addition to a few dollars. I went to the grocery store and purchased a few items. I carried them to Ruth's house and all of the children were happy to see me. They grabbed the bags, removed the items, and said with excitement, "*beans, peas, rice, corn and chicken!*" I was excited because they were so cheerful. I did not have much but I shared what I had. I returned to my little place with peace of mind.

Many nights I retired for bed without a meal. People have often said history repeats itself, but I did not expect it to happen so soon. I generally ate lunch at work but some days the food was just plain lousy. We did not have very much food at home. Surprise! surprise! My roommate and I returned home after a day's work. Really, to our surprise there were two men in our apartment. They had entered through the rear door, cooked food, and served themselves! They had nerves to crawl into our beds and go to sleep. They were men whom Jezebel knew. I was furious and had every right to be. We soon got rid of them. Before they left, I talked about them as if they had stolen something and they really had. *They ate our food!*

"They should be arrested for invasion of privacy," I said.

"Oh! No, they my friends," Jezebel said.

"Some friends they are!," I replied.

"I cannot handle that type of company, they are thieves," I continued.

Impromptu Decision and Results

On one occasion when it was raining very hard, a down pour. I was not feeling well and experiencing horrible stomach cramps. It was the end of our eight-hour shift and time to go home. We really did not want to wait for the bus. I made the mistake of telling Jezebel where Romeo lived. It was a short distance from work. Jezebel insisted that we walk over. When we arrived, *she asked* Romeo to carry us home. He did just that and he got to know Jezebel as well. She removed her blouse and walked around in the apartment in her bra. I suppose she wanted to show off her *big breasts*. That was some demonstration before a man, who she never saw before. I went to my room and got into bed because I was in much pain. I left Romeo in the front room of the apartment with Jezebel. I do not know what time he left the apartment.

It was late one night and there was a knock at the door. Jezebel answered. Romeo was there. This time he had not been invited to my knowledge. Maybe Jezebel decided that she wanted to see him. He said he had been to Freeman & Harris Café and decided to stop by. Oh, but I wondered why. I returned to my room. After all, I was scheduled to work the following day. I did not discuss the matter with Jezebel, who was probably up to no good. The next morning I went to work as usual. She did not go to work that day and a few days later, she told me she had spent time with Romeo. I bet she did. It sounded like a plan to me. She was a Jezebel. Apparently, she did not like the expression on my face.

"We ain't friends," She said boldly, as she walked away.

Months later Jezebel was laid off her job. Thank God, she moved back with her parents. Before she left another co-worker named, Helen moved with me. She was very different from the first one and from the second one too. That was a relief. I could breathe a little easier and I felt safe. I thought, "Now I can relax, Helen seems to be the right one."

Attempted Rape

One afternoon while I was relaxing in bed one of Jezebel's associates came by unexpectedly. Helen had walked down the hallway to the bathroom. Unfortunately, she left the door unlocked. Mr. Bad Guy walked in and found me in bed. The monster attempted to rape me. Surely, he did not think I was a little Jezebel. However, he found out quickly and we fought for a while. The monster ripped my *beautiful, ruffled, light blue nightgown,* but I managed to get out of bed. The man was reacting as if he were insane. He was perspiring heavily, and his eyes were really big and white! I was scared half to death, but I did not dare let him know that. Helen returned during the struggle and told him to leave but he just yelled at her. He picked up a chair from the kitchen table and used it to jam me against the wall while holding the legs of the chair around me.

"Will you pl-e-a-s-e leave?," Helen asked, as if she were afraid.

Finally, he left in a hurry as if he was going to put out a fire and maybe he was. I concluded that he would not use me! Strangely, he had a wife and children. That did not seem to matter. I was aware of the fact that he had been there before, only to visit with Jezebel. She should have notified all her friends that she had moved out! A police officer came by and I gave him all the information. I also summoned my property owner who in turn said she would see that the *"would-be rapist"* stay away from the apartment. Helen was laid off her job. She moved with her sister and again I was left alone.

"Is this good or bad?," I asked myself.

I did not have the answer, but I was going through a *chain of storms.* I found another job because the administrators were downsizing at Gown's Sanitarium. That time I worked at Hell Hounds Nursing Home. Thank God I was paid a small percentage more. I worked like a Hebrew slave and there was always something to be done. Work, work, work, feed the patients, assist them with dressing themselves, clean their bedrooms, and bathe them even if they were to be showered in their wheelchairs. I performed many duties even in the laundry room. I was trying to earn my living and not take advantage of anyone. Co-workers were not always nice either. Most of them knew that I was struggling to make it all by myself. I had no other income and it was difficult to meet my needs with the small salary. I was not blessed with a savings account from which, I could withdraw funds when times were tough. They really were tough! I had no transportation therefore; I was not able to work an additional job. I really did not want to be away from home at night, especially since I had to ride the trolley.

Mr. Smarty came to my rescue. He asked many questions and gave me advice too. I considered him to be a father figure. He assured me that he had much experience as an adult. However, he had a hidden agenda and he called me a little *"Indian girl."*

Esther purchased a red and white plaid blanket for me. She brought it to me because she knew I was struggling to survive. It was certainly needed and I thanked her and God for the blessing!

Sometimes when people know you are in need, they are likely to take advantage of you. I have been there and it's grievous! There are some lions in this world so to speak. They are not all in the jungle, neither are they contained in cages. I cried many nights because I had no one to turn to. I knew the heartaches of living from day to day with scarce funds or no funds at all. As I look back over my life and think things over, I realize I can identify with those who lived during the *"great depression."* As I look at the immense profile of my life, I recognize the fact that I was so immature, or 'green' is the word, which I have heard older people use. Only during that time, I did not understand and I had no wisdom. However, time has brought about changes. I thank God for the trials. I am now able to withstand the strong winds. I indeed had some *wilderness experiences*. I thank God for the storms He brought me through! The Lord knows they were rough, but I stood the test! I stood alone so many times and I cried just as many!

Rose Marie

I often wonder how Mom's second child died, and where she is buried. I am inquisitive. I think about her often. As I grow older, I have more in-depth thoughts about the little girl. One day I called Ruth and we talked.

"Do you know how Rose Marie was buried and where? Does her grave have a headstone?," I asked out of concern.

"She was so little, they put her in a shoe box for burial," Ruth answered. "I don't know where they buried her, and I don't know anything about a headstone," She added after a moment of silence.

"The little baby wasn't even buried in a casket. There are caskets for babies too," I replied.

Then I recalled something, which I heard someone say. "Rose Marie's body was placed in an apple crate." I thought, "Oh, my God! Maybe after placing her body in the shoe box, it was placed in an apple crate, which served the purpose of an outer casket."

After that thought, my imagination was really magnified. It was time for an interrogation.

"Where was Rose Marie buried?," I called and asked Dad.

"We wer' living on Mr. Neely's Place in Grand Bayou. We buried the baby in the back yard of the house whar we were living," He told me as if it was no big deal.

I could hardly believe I heard him right.

"She was just a few days old and so lit-t-le," He continued.

"She should have been buried in a casket, and it should not have mattered how small she was," I said with emphasis.

"Well, that's whar' we buried her, He said in a nonchalant tone.

I was sad. My mind quickly went back to the days of the "task master." Dad did not care about anybody. He did not say he was unable to bury the baby properly.

"What was the cause of death?," I asked.

"Her mama had a fever when she was car' her and the baby had a fever," Dad said, dragging his words.

"Okay," I said.

That conversation was over. I was astonished. I had never heard anyone say Mom had a fever when she lost the child. There were so many unanswered questions. Mom kept important papers in an old purse, but I never saw a death certificate for a baby. Most likely, it was never obtained. It is sad to say, but there seems to be no one to put my mind at ease. Surely, there is no need to ponder over such things. However, specific questions crossed my mind as I reminisced. Rose Marie was a newborn baby who entered into this world and quickly made her exit.

I used my vivid imagination.

I am aware that from the tree of life each leaf must fall, the green and gold, the great and the small. As I concluded, she was characterized as a small *"green leaf."* She was in the very early season of life, spring. It is needless to say, but it was the dawn of her life. I continued to think and roll back the curtain of time in my mind. I used my imagination and immediately, but clearly observed a tiny rosebud. It was little and wrapped so securely. Yet it displayed, exposed, or revealed a beautiful ray of color. It was a remarkable sight while just waiting to unfold. Perhaps, it would have blossomed into a lovely flower, but no, it was chosen while just a tiny, tiny rosebud. I can imagine that special rosebud in the midst of a garden of colorful flowers. It has been given a unique name and it shall live forever.

The Aftermath of Death

Without doubt, I knew Mom was sad for a while, but she knew of such is the kingdom of heaven, and children are gifts from God. Even with such knowledge I am certain she felt like a broken vessel, and desired the Potter to put her back together again. God is able to mend a broken heart. When He gathers the pieces of a broken vessel, He mends it and leaves no sign of the smallest crack. Only He is able to perform such a miraculous job. He is the Potter and we are the clay. He is able to mold us and make us after His will. Many times, we face the unexpected. Such was the case with Mom. We realize that sometimes we must release our beloved children to start a new and different life, the fifth season. I am sure many mothers can attest that it is not easy. Even though Mom's little one had just made her arrival, she did not tarry but went to be with the Lord. The door was open for her and after she entered, it was closed behind her. Mom had to accept the fact and continue her journey. We know God is able to fill the void in our lives after deaths, tragedies, and all calamities. God is the Great I am…

We must continue to put our trust in Him. The Psalmist reminded us, *it is better to trust in the Lord than to put confidence in man.*

Psalm 118:8 (KJV)

I was still curious. I wondered, "Whom would Rose Marie resemble if she were here today? Would she be tall and slender like Dad, or of short stature with big hips like Mom? Would she be mean and cruel or meek and humble?" Those are questions, which cannot be answered. Reality is she quickly escaped the harsh treatments, which the rest of us endured. Sometimes I think it is best not to know or experience certain things. Job spoke of infants, which never saw light. He said, "The small and great are there; (in death) and the servant is free from his master."

Leah, Rebekah and Dinah

The three girls lived together and they went to school together. They even found themselves in trouble together. Rebekah is Ruth's daughter. Leah and Dinah are my sisters. Ruth came face to face with a substantial challenge. She worked daily in the private home of Mrs. Wealthy. It was a big responsibility to care for four sisters and three children of her own. I had my own place so she was not concerned about me. One who has always had plenty may not be able to fathom the financial stress. However, Ruth dealt with the responsibility of discipline, the hardship of dealing with complaints of peer pressure, and total survival.

It was Friday night and the girls asked to go to the neighborhood park. Ruth gave them permission to go.

"Be back home at 10:00 P.M.," Ruth gave the girls instructions.

The three girls went to the recreation center. They loved to dance. Leah was the star attraction. She could dance and she got the attention of the others. Rebekah could not dance; she really went along to *try to keep Leah in line*. Moreover, Leah thought she really had it "*going on*." The girls were among other teenagers and they were having a good time.

Rebekah was wearing the timepiece and she was expected to alert Leah and Dinah when it was time to leave the center. Apparently, she was caught up in the action and did not realize her watch had stopped. Others were leaving the premises. Surprisingly it was not 10:00 O' clock. It was 12:00 midnight. They were two hours late. The dance was over and it was time to close the recreation center. The "*dance trio*" was in serious trouble. They made their way home in a hurry only to be denied entrance into the house. They knocked on the door.

"Who is it?," Ruth asked very angrily.
"Let us in," Rebekah responded.
"What time y'all think it is?," Ruth asked angrily.

Leah and Dinah allowed Rebekah to communicate with Ruth. Perhaps they underestimated her. They though she would let her own daughter into the house but not so. She did not that time.

"We know it's late, but...", Rebekah said.
"I don't know where y'all going, but you ain't coming in here,"

Ruth interrupted Rebekah as she tried to explain their plight, but Ruth refused to listen. Simultaneously the girls pleaded to be let inside. Ruth ignored them. It was past their curfew and they had violated her rule. She refused to open the door and she would not hear their explanation. The trio sat down on the driveway.

"Get off my property," Ruth shouted.

They walked to the end of the driveway and sat down again. Ruth told them she would shoot her gun if they did not leave. Apparently, the trio took her seriously after that statement. Maybe she would have fired the gun. Ruth became known as *"shot gun Annie."* She really could be mean sometimes. She was still young and afraid to allow room for mistakes. Leah was stubborn and had a mind of her own.

"Leah is going to do what Leah wants to do," She said in a sassy tone.

She knew that Ruth would *use the belt* on them but that did not faze her. One morning, Ruth did just that and accidentally hit Leah in the eye. She was admitted in Confederate Memorial. I went to visit her and she had partially removed the eye patch so she could see anyway. Her eye was supposed to be covered completely. Soon, she was released from the hospital. She did things her way.

"Leah told us, a whipping don't last long," Dinah said.
"She popped her fingers and strolled around like nothing mattered," Dinah continued.
The girl was left-handed and carefree! The trio decided to go to Esther's house, which was not far from the recreation center. They walked over to her home expecting to be invited inside. They knocked on her door and told her their problem.

"Ruth didn't let you into her house, so I ain't gonna let you into mine," Said Esther. They were very disappointed and it was late.

I lived on Cox Street in a little duplex house. It was not very far from Esther's house. All of a sudden, I heard footsteps then a knock at the door. It was late and I did not have the slightest idea who was there. To my surprise, it was Leah, Dinah and Rebekah, the dance trio. They were on the run like fugitives and had become like the *"three little pig."* They were running from house to house in search of shelter. My place was their third stop but it certainly was not a brick house. I open the door and they gladly entered. I can truly say they were relieved to find shelter. What a nightmare! They explained why they were out so late, found a quilt, and curled up on the floor the remainder of the night. It was a night to be remembered! They went home the next day. I do not know if they explained to Ruth where they spent the night.

Rebekah and Dinah shared the same bed at Ruth's home. One night Rebekah got into bed not with Dinah but with an uninvited guest. She said suddenly there was movement beneath her body. She felt something wiggle but she did not dare get up to investigate. I thought that was strange. Instead, she remained very still and as snug as a bug in a rug, but she was somewhat frightened. She said finally, there was no movement beneath her. She fell asleep and slept all night. To her surprise the next morning, she discovered her guest, *"a mouse."* He had gotten into the wrong place at the wrong time and was no doubt smothered to death. The little creature had made his way onto a comfortable warm spot only to be killed. He was unable to wiggle his way out from beneath the weight of Rebekah's body. As a result, he faced death. He would not play his game again and neither would he be missed. Then she had the task of removing the dead mouse and of course, his final resting place was not a cemetery but the city dump! No one wept for him and no one said farewell. It was good riddance!

Rebekah probably said, "You shouldn't have been in my bed."

Preparing to clean the Cemetery @ Grand Bayou, La.

News Bulletin

In the late 1960s, Mr. John Moss, P.E instructor and four residents of Coushatta, Louisiana were killed in a fiery auto crash on highway 1.

Chapter 12

Mission Accomplished

1968 & 1970
Anna and Lois graduated from Union High School. It is now a Medical Career Center. Commencement Exercises were held at eight o'clock in the Municipal Auditorium.

1971
I successfully challenged the exam to work for a local telephone company. I was hired. During the weeks of training, my instructor was a young Caucasian woman. She was not very nice! She seemed to have formed an opinion about me before we began. The supervisor was an older woman who apparently was in need of an attitude adjustment also.

"These two employees seem to have a problem with my being here," I said. "I need a job, and God blessed me to be here, so I am going to focus on the training," I said.

The Training
I was given a book to read and the instructor expected me to demonstrate what I read.
After I told my cousin Rachel about the training, she said, "Good gracious, that is a lot to learn."
I replied, "That is just one segment of the training."
There was RO (Reach Operator)

DA (Directory Assistance)
Busy and Local Emergency

I was given a number of area code to memorize. The most complicate task was learning to work with *"coin telephones."* The sound of a quarter was Bong. The sound of a nickel was Bing and the sound of a dime was Bing, Bing. I was expected to know all the information and apply it professionally without making mistakes. When a mistake was made, no explanation was good enough.

The trainer told me, "Be on time and if a train is in your pathway find an alternate route." She continued, "Put your headset on and be at the keyboard at the start of your shift." She was more than strict. She was harsh, a second place pharaoh! At the end of the shift I was tired mentally, exhausted, and really stressed out.

"Is this job really worth it?,' I asked myself.

I had experienced a *storm of rejection.*
One day I was on my way to work when the brakes failed on my car. I thank God for keeping me safe. I did not have an accident. Right then I quickly concluded, "This job is not for me." After a lengthy conversation with the supervisor, I resigned and immediately felt relieved. I should have told her *whatsoever a man soweth, that shall he also reap.*

Galatians 6:7 (KJV)

"I had applied twice for a job with the phone company. I was determined to work there," I told a friend.

"You will find another job," She responded, trying to encourage me.

I learned a lesson. We need to ask God for guidance before we attempt to do anything. Some things are not meant to be for some people. When we try our best and things do not work out, perhaps God has something else for us. We make plans but God *finalizes* them.

1972, Leah graduated from Woodlawn High School. Commencement Exercises were held Tuesday evening, May 23 at eight o'clock in Hirsch Memorial Center. She made her home in Shreveport, Louisiana, and held various jobs before coming face to face with *multiple medical problems.* She had two sons, whom she loved dearly. Leah was very protective of her baby boy, whom she referred to as *"my man."* Her older son brought much joy into her life by playing football during his high school years.

All Grown-up

Anna worked for Western Electric before she and her fiancé decided to tie the knot. They exchanged vows at Calvary Baptist Church. Reverend Richard Kessee did the honors. They relocated to Dallas, Texas and she and *hubby* have two children, a daughter, Lisa who resembles her dad, and a son, Ced who resembles his mom! Anna works in the healthcare field.

Lois relocated to Dallas, Texas and found work in a factory. She met Mr. *Good bar.* The couple tied the knot and they have a set of twins, a girl, Timi, and a son, Rere. Lois works in the healthcare field also.

Dinah, our baby sister graduated from Woodlawn High School. She went off to college at Northwestern State University in Natchitoches, Louisiana. Later, she and her fiancé made a decision to get married. I fashioned a beautiful gown for her. Dinah married Lance, the *tall, dark, and handsome,* love of her life at New Star Baptist Church. The couple has three beautiful daughters, Tabitha, Serena, and Mariah. After ten years, Dinah and family relocated to Dallas, Texas. They are members of Hopewell Baptist Church where Dinah is very active. She serves as a teacher with the Children and Youth Department. She currently works as a *refund* specialist for a major company.

Our mom would be very proud of all of us. Ruth is elated! She has done an excellent job and kept her promise to Mom. There were many times when darkness closed in by way of medical and financial problems. The way was not easy but liken to that of a *roller coaster.*

Speaking Metaphorically

Storms, storms, and more storms raged. Strong winds blew and kept on blowing. Rain fell, but we endeavored to survive. Sometimes it seemed as if we were to either *sink or swim.* Those who could breaststroke made it to shore. Others grabbed whatever was within their reach in order to make it to safety. Life was just that hard! However, God saw us through the storms. To God be the glory for the things He has done!

Directions

Ruth is not our mom but she stepped up to the plate after Mom passed away. All parents may learn a lesson from the Eagles, which are symbols of freedom and power. They are noted for their strength. The Eagle feeds and protects her young but also teaches them to fly solo and survive. Having taught them, she set herself apart from them.

Biological parents, foster parents, or godparents nurture children and they are given directions to travel the highways of life. Many have been shown the "*brick walls*" of trouble. Parents hope their children will observe them and make the appropriate detour in a timely manner. Sometimes instructions, which are given, are ignored. Because of disobedience, *children injure themselves.* They should be cognizant that they are never smarter than their parents are wise. In essence, we must learn when to space ourselves from our children. They must learn to be survivors and stand on their own two feet.

Ruth was still very young and she did not give us the lessons, which an aged person would have given us, but we were able to grasp some information on our own. There comes a time when each must go his separate way. Thus, we set out to accomplish our goals and find our places in life. God has given all of us talents. We must discover and utilize them to the best of our abilities. When God bless us, we are expected to be a blessing to our fellow man. We are our *brother's keeper.*

Solomon penned the book of Proverbs. He reminds us to consider the ways of an ant and be wise. The little creature has no guide, overseer, or ruler. This means they do not need a taskmaster. They are wise enough to prepare for hard times. Solomon informed us that the ant provides her meat in the summer, and gathers her food in the harvest. This tells us that the ant works in the summer thereby; she has food for the winter. We are fearfully and marvelously made in the image of God and we must be wise, work, and care for ourselves.

We had a rough start. In this life, there are mountains, valleys, raging storms and many obstacles to overcome. No one ever said this *pilgrimage* would be one of ease. However, what matters most is how we finish the race. We learned ways to survive as time passed. The school of Hard

Knocks displayed an extremely hard curriculum, but if one is nurtured with care before shown the rugged road, he will survive.

The Work Place

July 16, 1973

I started to work at Confederate Memorial Medical Center as a laboratory technical assistant II. As I reflect on the first few weeks at work, the job was demanding. The requirements were that one *must have college credits and successfully challenge the civil service examination.* That meant a test score was necessary. Applicants were hired and informed of the requirements. If they were not met within a period, employees were terminated. Standards were high and employees were knowledgeable. Before I had a chance to challenge the examination, a heavyset man, who was partially bald-headed, confronted me with a card for union membership. He reminded me several times to become a member. He did not know if I were prepared to challenge the test. Furthermore, he did not ask. He was trying to recruit *union members.*

On September 18, 1973, I passed the test for my position. The exam was given at Vocational Technical Institute in Shreveport, Louisiana. The job was said to be secure at that point.

Confederate Memorial is the hospital where the grey-haired, mean Caucasian woman worked in 1965. My mother was there as a patient. Some of the employees seemed to have a preconceived opinion of others. Therefore, I was not eager to work there. However, I was thankful for the opportunity. My husband was employed there and we have two children. My salary was $350.00 per month and employees were paid on the fifth and 20th of each month. *That was not fair!*

My duties ranged from performing venipunctures and capillary sticks to cleaning countertops in the work area. There was a lack of space and we did not have the best equipment. Needles did not have the rubber tip over the end that was placed into the vacutainer. Therefore, the vacutainer filled with blood when multiple specimens were collected. My lab coat was sprinkled with blood sometimes. Personal protective equipment was neither available nor required to be utilized. Were it not for the grace and mercy of God I could have become infected via contaminated blood.

I explained hardships to my children. I went to work early and Ruth carried the girls to school. Sari was five years old. She attended kindergarten at Caddo Heights Elementary School. I told her that she was a big girl because I did not want her to cry. Lydia went to Fairfield Daycare Center, which was not far from Sari's school. Every night I combed the girls' hair and tied a silk scarf around each one's head. I laid their clothes and socks out. Lunch money was tied in a handkerchief and pinned to each girl's dress the old fashioned way. They ate cereal or grits for breakfast.

I prayed to God to protect my children and allow me to live to see them grow up. I taught them to say their prayers every night. They prayed the little children's prayer of "*lay me down to sleep.*" As they grew, I taught them to pray the "*model prayer,*" which Jesus taught his disciples to pray.

Sari could not remember how to put her shoes on correctly. I placed them together on the floor and drew a curved line inside each shoe.

"The curved lines look like a broken circle when the shoes are together right," I said to Sari." That is the way you should put them on," I continued.
One day Sari went to school wearing her shoes on the wrong feet and Kim Collins noticed them.

"Do they hurt?," asked Kim.
"Yeah they hurt," Sari replied.
"When they hurt that mean you have them on the wrong feet," Kim said.
Sari finally got them right. It took another child to get her to understand.

She was a girl scout, and that was the beginning of activities. Sari was as cute as a button when she adorned her little green uniform. She had her Girl Scout book and she sold cookies as most girls do. She and Lydia took piano lessons, which were taught by Mr. Walters. I purchased many music books from Perry's Book Store.

We carried the girls to Sunday school on Sundays and each summer they went to Vacation Bible School. On May 6, 1976, Sari was baptized at Paradise Baptist Church.

September 17, 1976, I purchased my first automobile for $5,814.06. My monthly payment was $138.43. It was a white Mustang with red interior and a hatchback door. I applaud Mr. Richard Spikes, the black man who invented the *automatic gearshift*. He certainly made it convenient for many others and me.

November 9, 1976, I successfully challenged the examination for a Laboratory Technical Assistant III. Shortly thereafter, I was motivated to challenge another. On December 12, 1978, I did very well on the Clerk I & II exam.

Lydia came home from Caddo Heights School with a box of world's finest *chocolate candy* bars. She intended to sell the candy for her school. The price was $1.00 per bar. To my surprise, two bars of candy were open. Lydia had taken a bite off each one. I knew those two were mine. *I had to pay for them.* I gave her instructions not to open another bar of candy.

"You cannot sell them if they are open, and you must give the money to your teacher," I explained.
"Do you understand?," I asked Lydia.
"Yes, mama," Lydia replied.

She sold her candy and she followed my instructions. She followed her sister in school activities. Lydia loved Vacation Bible School, she confessed Christ, and was baptized on June 19, 1977. She sang beautifully and played the piano. Her favorite song was, "*my liberty.*

I returned to work. One day I was informed of the medical library. The room contained medical history of patients. I immediately began to search for information concerning my mother, Annie B. Clarkson-Turner. I found it. The history revealed that Mom was *terminally ill*. I was astonished. I paused for a moment. My mind quickly traveled back in time, and it seemed to be as dark as a thousand midnights. Suddenly, I felt a sense of loneliness and *grief*. I reflected on the moment that I received the news that *Mom was gone*. After a moment, I snapped out of my daze and began to read the history. I was shocked and baffled.

"What happened to informed consent," I wondered.
"Today is the first day of the rest of my life and I must go on," I reminded myself.

"Dear God, please give me strength and courage to begin again," I prayed.

I called Ruth and informed her about my findings.

"Well, we can't do nothing about it," She replied.

She was so nonchalant. I knew I could not change what happened, but I deserved some answers. An unprecedented chapter had been written in my life.

It was summer and the girls wanted to go to six flags in Arlington, Texas. Their dad and I prepared to take them. Sari and Lydia were as happy as two peas in a pod! They grabbed their pillows and Lydia got her little stuffed animal to take with her.

One said to the other, "O' yeah, we are going to ride on the big caterpillar and..." I interrupted, "You cannot ride everything by yourself."

I continued, "I will make the decision about what you can ride."

They were quiet for a while. Finally, Sari said, "Mama you can ride with me and Dad can ride with Lydia." I had told her that she was a big girl, but she was not that big. I did not need her to work things out for me. We put our bags into the car and left for Arlington. The girls chatted a while then Lydia fell asleep. When we arrived at the hotel, Sari said repeatedly, "Wake up Lydia, we're getting ready to go and ride." She was so excited she could hardly contain herself. Once we were on the grounds, we walked around to observe what was available first. We enjoyed the excitement and the food was good. We returned to our room and the next day we headed home to Shreveport.

Back on the job...

I collected blood samples the in intensive care units and on the polio ward. I became aware of the iron lung. I never imagined seeing a patient in such a device. The iron lung was used to treat paralysis of the muscles and organs of breathing.

In 1978, the name Confederate Memorial Medical Center was changed to Louisiana State University Health Sciences Center.

My great aunt became ill and I carried her to see the physician of her choice, Doctor Lee. She lived with my family and me several weeks. She was happy with us and I took care of her. When her condition worsened I

139

continued to keep her in my home before she was hospitalized. Her health continued to fail. The physicians discussed amputating one of her feet. Aunt Matt disagreed with the doctors' decision.

"Your doctor said you cannot survive without the surgery," I explained.

"Let me take all of my bones with me," Auntie said, reassuring me that she meant what she said.

Doctor Ales looked at me and said, *"Place her in a nursing home."*

He indicated that he was not going to do anything else for her because she refused the surgery. Aunt Matt was very ill and I did not want to put her through surgery against her will.

I called Ruth and informed her about Auntie's condition.

"If it will prolong her life, *let them do it*," She said.

Auntie was 79 years old. I just *could not* sign the paper to amputate her foot.

"I ain't gonna worry you much longer," She said, as if she knew what was happening.

"All my things will be yours one day and you can do whatever you want to do with them," She continued.

She told me how to handle her business. We discussed her burial policy, final resting place, and color of clothing for burial. She even talked about her church. She had her business in order. She did not have any living children. Her only child, a son passed away when he was a young man. He had one son who passed away as a child.

January 20, 1979 was a Saturday. That night I had a dream. Aunt Matt was a little girl. Her hair was combed back and in one braid. She was lying on her back halfway underneath a fence. When I woke up, I was concerned. It was Sunday morning and I decided to attend morning service first, then I went to the hospital to visit Auntie. She had been removed all the way to the end of the ward. I entered the room on 8G and I knew immediately that Auntie was gone. She had aspirated and passed away. No one had gone into the room to check on her. *The staff was not aware that she was dead.*

Aunt Matt passed away on January 21, 1979. I contacted Saint Rest Baptist Church and made the funeral arrangements according to her wishes. Mr. Wishbone did not want to give me the $250.00, which was in a bank downtown. Finally, he said, "Aren't you going to give me something?" I needed every bit of the $250.00 to take care of her business. Opening and closing the grave cost was $90.00 alone, and I prepared to place a headstone on her grave.

Her brother, Scarborough had passed away five years earlier (March 21, 1974). Both were laid to rest in Carver Memorial Cemetery. Aunt Matt was the last one of several sisters and brothers. They were grandma, Dolly's siblings.

June 1979, I was still classified as a laboratory tech assistant. We were told we would no longer centrifuge blood samples. Suddenly, we were told we would be reallocated. Out title was changed to phlebotomy technicians. That was a *downgrade and an injustice* to all who met the qualifications for laboratory technical assistant. The standards were altered to accommodate others.

"We worked to change things, no test is needed," Said the union president. That was not right. We were not given a choice to either keep the title, which we earned or accept the lower position. But others showed no concern because they were not affected by the changes. Many were reluctant to advise me how to handle the problem. However, I made it through the unfair changes. I realize that many things in life are not fair. There are some in positions at the top of ladder, but they will not make corrections. I told God about my problems and I taught my girls to pray for whatever they need. We must first *acknowledge* God, *confess* our sins, *thank Him* for everything, and *petition* God for our needs.

It was summer and the girls were out of school. We went to Walt Disney World on vacation. It was an interesting trip. Sightseeing was fascinating and we saw the Florida Orange Groves. We brought back lots of pictures, *magic kingdom passports*, and tour guides as keepsakes. Tabitha is my niece. She was excited to accompany us on the trip. Our hotel room was filled with laughter every night. The girls reminisced about cartoon characters. Lydia was the center of attention. She talked about Tom and Jerry.

"Baby mouse told his uncle a *pussy cat* was in the room," said Lydia.
"Uncle did not believe him," She continued.
Baby mouse told his uncle, "I did see a *pus-sy cat*, I did, I did," said Lydia.

The girl laughed and I laughed until I cried.

April 19, 1985, I was blessed with back pay as the result of a court case XXP versus the Department of State Civil Service. My check *exceeded one grand*. That was a blessing from God. Not everyone in the department received a check.

In June, we went to Hot Springs, Arkansas. Sari and Lydia wanted to ride on the big yellow duck, an *amphibious bus*. Their dad was willing to go sightseeing, but I was somewhat hesitant.

"Can we go Mama?,"Sari said.
"Yes, let's ride on the duck," Said Lydia
I agreed, "Ok, girls."
Everything was fine until the duck approached the Hamilton Lake.
"O', no!," I cried.
"I am not ready for this," I continued, as I looked across the enormous lake.
"It's safe. I have been doing this for years," The driver said.
"But I was not one of your passenger," I said.
"Do you have life jackets?," I asked.
"Yes, but we have never had a need to use them," He stated.

He proceeded to drive into the lake. I was apprehensive, but the girls cheered, "Y-a-h."
Lydia leaned forward and tried to touch the water.

"*No*, don't do that," I cried.

Both girls had taken swimming lessons at the Young Women's Christian Association. They did fine, but the lake was not the place to practice. As the amphibious bus toured the lake, I was silent. Soon we were back on dry land and I was delighted.

"Thank you Lord," I said. I should have known the duck would go into water somewhere. We did not dare go on another tour. There had been enough excitement. I definitely have a fear of large bodies of water (hydrophobia). It did not dawn on me that we were going into a lake. I would have told the girls we were not going on the tour. We returned home.

We did not travel much after the trip to Hot Springs. We carried the girls to Crystal Palace to skate on Saturdays, and sometimes we went to Dallas, Texas to visit family.

Sari

Sari was very active in school. *She sang in the choir,* participated on the drill team, and on flag line. She was the *director* for the youth choir at Shady Grove Baptist Church #1 and Lydia was the *musician.* Sari was also a member of Reserve Officers Training Corp. I fashioned most of her clothes including her military ball gown, senior prom dress, and etc. Sari was a debutante and she was one of the first students of the *medical career* magnet class. She graduated from high school with honors and planned to go to nursing school. Suddenly, Sari decided to go to the United States Navy. I was disappointed. However, she packed her bags and went to Orlando, Florida for training. *Basic training was hard and the rules were stringent.* She called home crying, I encouraged her, and prayed for her.

She made it through the hard times and traveled cross-country. Sari was activated for operation *desert storm*. She traveled to San Diego, California. She returned home safely. Thank God. She presently works as a nurse at Dallas Regional Medical Center.

Lydia received recognition for outstanding accomplishments at Linwood middle school. She was also *yearbook queen*. At Woodlawn high school, she received an award from zeta iota zeta chapter. She was recognized for outstanding scholastic achievements, qualities of finer womanhood, and the determination to excel. Lydia was a debutante for Christ. She graduated with honors, continued her education at Grambling State University, and graduated with a degree in computer information systems. She is employed at Caddo Parish School Board as a child nutrition bookkeeper.

I am thankful to God for my children. They had a well-rounded childhood. They did not participate in sleepovers with friends because I was responsible for their well-being. I did not want to have reasons to worry about what was going on in another woman's home. The girls did not agree with my decision, but I am the parent! Now, they have children and they understand. Thank God.

Untimely Deaths & Events

October 03, 1986, I was informed of the death of a cousin. Brian Rayburn Turner was killed instantly in a fiery crash when his car slammed into an 18-wheeler in Red River Parish. He was pronounced dead at the scene. Apparently, he was in route to his resident in Shreveport. He died sixteen days before his twenty-third birthday.

1986-10-03 Date of Death
<u>1963-10-19 Date of Birth</u>
    22-11-14 Age at time of Death

I recall Brian's father, Harry W. Turner was also killed in an automobile accident. He died three days after his thirty-fifth birthday. Father and son were *killed in the months in which they were born*. We cherish their memory.

1977-08-26 Date of Death
<u>1942-08-23 Date of Birth</u>

35-00-03 Age at time of Death

In 1990, my immediate supervisor retired. I had gone through many *unfair changes*. They may be likening to *wilderness experiences*. However, I was promoted to phlebotomy supervisor. I held the position sixteen years.

In 1992

Mark Flames returned home after twenty-nine years. Family and friends met at Rebekah's home and we had much to discuss. Mr. Flames had returned from his cross-country journey. Although he reminded me of the biblical story of the prodigal son, no one brought forth the best robe and put it on him. No one put a ring on his finger, or shoes on his feet. In addition, no one killed the fatted calf that he could eat and be merry. However, we did celebrate with food. It was a joyous time for some, a reminder for several, and a *time of awakening for others*.

The truth was brought to light. I believe *the traveler* was convicted by his own conscience. He did not dare communicate with certain family members. Perhaps he was evasive for fear of what the conversations might entail. Surely, he was cognizant of his *improper conduct.* He should have felt ashamed! However, he posed for photos with his children and others as if everything was in order.

A homecoming celebration was held at Mount Olive Baptist Church, Grand Bayou, Louisiana on July 05, 1992 at 4:00 p.m. Many family members attended and some did not. Mr. Flames two grandchildren were asked to welcome him back home. Reverend Charlie Henry was expected to deliver the sermon. He was not available, but Reverend Wardell did the honors. Mr. Flames was asked to make remarks. We expected him to explain his long absence, or at least apologize. It did not happen. He did not say much about anything, and no one knew what was going through his mind.

Poem, "A Second Chance"

A second chance to *see clearly,*
A second chance to *think sincerely,*
A second chance to *be dearly,*
A second chance to *speak freely,*
A second chance to *start all over again,*
A second chance to *pass God's test,*

A second chance to *do my very best.*

By: Gwendolyn Lubom-Foster

1992

Used by permission

January 31, 1995

My family surprised me with a birthday party at Freeman & Harris Café. My siblings, Sari, and Lydia were able to make plans without my knowledge of what was going on. I had gotten dressed in my navy blue pantsuit and I adorned a navy hat with a gold band. That was the usual for me. I went by Ruth's house and I noticed Anna and others were there from Dallas, but I did not suspect anything. When Lydia said, "Mama don't go home and eat, we are taking you out for dinner. I simply said ok. Then I thought about it. When we arrived at the café, I saw many family members and I was sure it was meant to be a surprise. The food was delicious and several brought gifts to me. The cake was quite different and a big surprise. Gwendolyn and Deborah purchased beautiful, musical, birthday cards, which contained heartwarming messages. They are keepsakes.

Family Reunion

June 14-16, 2002

The Clarkson-Turner Family Reunion was held in Shreveport. On Friday, June 14, Yvette opened the doors of her home to the family for a party. Saturday the 15th we met at Betty Virginia Park for a picnic of fun, games, and a show of talents. Food was plentiful and good! We wore light blue t-shirts and khaki pants for unity and posed for many photos. What a reunion it was. Family and friends came from far and near for a happy celebration. On Sunday, June 16, we met at Bright Morning Star Baptist Church at Abington, Louisiana for service. God brought us together once again and it was a happy occasion.

Ruth's Birthday

May 31, 2004

Ruth was sixty-five years old. Rachel was the host at her home for the birthday celebration. Family and friends enjoyed the special blessing. We enjoyed a variety of good food, which included fried catfish, boiled crawfish, corn on the cob, barbecue, and much more. We were thankful that God brought us together again for another happy occasion.

November 7, 2006

Auntie Susie celebrated her 80th birthday. Rachel, Miriam, and Samuel were elated. Their mom has lived four score years. It was a day of rejoicing and sharing with love ones. Friends and associates joined the great celebration. Auntie is happy to be among four generations. That is a blessing! Reggie fried catfish and others contributed a variety of dishes. We posed for photographs, which we hope to cherish many years. Rachel is overjoyed.

She has done and continues to do a marvelous job of caring for her mom. She shall be blessed.

June 21, 2008

My first book signing was held at Cedar Grove Branch Library. Family and friends gathered for the occasion. We continued the fellowship at Rachel's home, the ideal place for celebrating with food, taking pictures, and gathering information for *future references*. Support was overwhelming and I thank God for the opportunity, which allowed me to share with so many young relatives. Some were inquisitive while others enjoyed being present to share the blessing of the first book published by a family member. That is momentous. *"Define You!"* Is an inspirational book for all ages.

Family & Friends

February 12, 2010

It was Friday morning; Shreveport was covered with seven inches of snow. We had not seen such a beautiful, white blanket of snow in the city in a number of years. I received a phone call from Esther about 9:45 A.M. (CST)

"Hello, How you doing?," She asked.

"I am fine," I responded.

"How are you?," I continued.

"Oh, Praise the Lord Child, I'm doing good," She said.

"Have you been outside and washed your face with snow," She continued.

"No, I have not been outside," I answered.

"O' Child, Papa taught us to do that," She said as if it was a must-do thing.

"Papa always stored snow water in a bottle. He said it's good for *pink eye*," Esther stated.

"I do not remember that," I said.

"Well, sure thing 'cause Papa said so," She reminded me.

"Okay, you have a good day," She said.

Journey of Siblings

We started out on a sandy road, which led us through channels of turmoil. As we toiled on we reached the rocky trail, which led us through the *"valley of decisions."* After many days and nights of weighing the odds, we reached the base of the mountain. It was time to begin our upward climb. All of us at one time or another reached up to take hold of a ledge on the mountain. We hoped to pull ourselves up for a good start. As we stepped up from one hollow to another, sometimes there was danger lurking in our path. Decisions had to be made. However, all of us had to find our way of overcoming barriers. Sometimes that barrier was sickness. As I recall, not all sickness is until death. Many times the barrier was *disappointment, deception, rejection,* and even *loneliness.* We learned to look to Jesus for strength in our time of weakness. We prayed for guidance and we recalled God's Word is a lamp unto out feet and a light unto our path.

Today, as we continue to climb, we look for the next carved place. God gives us strength to brave the strong winds and grasp the next cliff. Some of our closest relatives have passed away. Each time we hesitated for a moment, or slowed our pace but kept traveling. As we scale the mountain, we see some who are unsaved. We must pause and share God's Word. We can stand on the rock. This rock is Jesus and He will support us. He is our strong tower. We are commissioned to share the *"plan of salvation"* with those in darkness. The Holy Spirit will bring to our remembrance that which we have studied. We must tell the unsaved, *"seek the Lord* while He may be found, call upon Him while He is near." Inform them, *there is none other name under heaven given among men, whereby we must be saved.*

Acts 4:12 (KJV)

Occasionally there is a wake up call, tragedy strikes. We are stunned and seem to freeze in our tracks. We must regain our focus, continue to travel, and be sure to place our feet on a sure foundation.

While moving on, we see some who are hungry. We must feed them. Some are naked and we must clothe them. God's Word teaches us, "*The poor we will have always.*" When we come face to face with the wayward travelers, we should not forget to give them a word of encouragement. We must not rush to reach the peak of success and bypass the opportunity to do important things. Neither should we look for short cuts. They may be pathways that are more rugged. When we notice a crowd afar off and they are traveling at a much faster pace, we should not be anxious to join them. That group may have warriors from all lifestyles. Some may be envious, eager to kick us off the cliff, and leave us for the wolves' pleasure with no compassion. I advise all to keep traveling on the narrow path, even though there are twists, turns, and very few pilgrims. Maintain a positive attitude and you will reach high altitudes. Place your feet carefully in each hollow. Perhaps it was carved with you in mind.

I am happy to report we are still endeavoring to make this journey. Ruth lives alone in the Hollywood Section of Shreveport, Louisiana. Despite her medical problems, she maintains her home and attends church regularly. She serves as an usher at New Star Baptist Church. Her children are adults and they have their own families and careers. Ruth's son is often by her side and he is supportive of her. Despite medical problems, he is blessed.

Esther lives in Greenbrook Subdivision of Shreveport, Louisiana. Her two sons live in Texas, and her daughter lives in Shreveport, Louisiana. Esther is a member of Union Springs Baptist Church.

Nevertheless, I must say our circle has been broken. Leah has gone home to be with the Lord and I am confident that she maintained a relationship with Him until the end. Time brought about many changes in her life. She made adjustments without complaining and endured much pain and suffering. Her two sons and grandchildren brought much happiness into her life. She endured the good and the bad. There were times when not all of us knew about every heartache. She chose not to share them. We prayed, prayed, and prayed for Leah.

However, Ruth stayed abreast of Leah's health concerns. She was there to lend a helping hand, give advice, and words of encouragement. Isaac and I were available to provide transportation to health care facilities, church and etc. Others shared our burden. We are thankful for them.

Lois was Leah's dear sister and late night communicator. As time passed, Leah experienced many diagnostic tests and surgeries. Family and friends were by her side often. During those last hours, I stood by her bedside, prayed, and assured her that everything was all right. She breathed her last breath. The life support machine drew a blank line and I closed her eyes knowing that chapter of her life was over. I was shaken to some degree, but God gave me the strength to stand the test. I did not shed one tear because I knew she had left the land of *"pain and suffering."* God knows she suffered!_Her debt has been paid in full!

"God is still in control," I said.

Even though I physically stood alone, yet I was not alone because my help was there. God and I are the majority!
What matters most is how Leah finished the race. She is happy because *...blessed are the dead, which die in the Lord...*

Revelation 14:13 (KJV)

From left to right: Dinah, Lois, Anna, Hannah, Esther, and Ruth

Sometimes the way seems to be so hard. Children are disobedient, Moms are too busy, and Fathers neglect their responsibilities. Thou the wind may blow, and the rain may fall on me, I am confident I shall get home someday! While the strong winds are blowing and we are tossed back and forth, we must be rooted in God's Word. We must ensure that our anchor holds and grips the solid rock. This rock is JESUS!

We may liken ourselves to evergreen trees, which do not change with the seasons and we must be planted on the good ground by our supplier.

And, he shall be planted by the rivers of water, that bringeth forth his fruit in his season; his leaf also shall not weather; and whatsoever he doeth shall prosper.

Psalm 1:3 (KJV)

Be not discouraged, but keep climbing until you reach your goal!
The storm will pass!
May God bless!